PARRIS FOTIAS

ADVENTURES THROUGH COVID

THE ART OF SUBCONSCIOUS TRAVEL IN A TRANSCENDENTAL STATE

 A catalogue record for this book is available from the National Library of Australia

australianauthors.store/parris-fotias/

Fotias, Parris (author)
Adventures Through COVID
ISBN 978-1-922629-56-2

Cover and book design by Green Hill Publishing

To all my friends in the travel industry. Despite
being routinely undervalued and systematically
overlooked, you inspire courage. This is just another
bump in the road and this too shall pass.

DESTINATION-ETA

CHAPTER 1
APRIL

123-456-789-458

Dear Diary,

I am officially back from leave and had a fabulous time away, although I will admit that I tried to cram too much into such a short time away. I should have listened to my travel agent, and now feel like I need another holiday.

At least I did get to visit all the sights on my bucket list, though: Kitchen, Backyard, Bedroom, Living Room, Dining Room. My only regret is that I didn't get to see the Laundry, although a few of my friends have said I didn't miss out on much. Oh well.

Anyway, now that I am back, I wonder how everyone is coping.

I do hope that they are keeping safe and well during these extremely unusual times. I keep letting them know that if they want to chat or vent, I can be contacted on my mobile. The fact that no one has called must mean they are in a good place.

Or maybe they just don't like me. Damn, I hadn't thought of that before. OK, just relax; and call your therapist once you finish this entry.

PS. My liquor stocks are still going strong. It certainly helps when you have a partner who doesn't drink much.

Dear Diary,

Another week, and I am still seeing those damn Dalgona coffee posts. No wonder everyone is so strung up and on edge. Decaf, people, decaf. With sincerest apologies to all my Victorian friends.

Anyway, I am due to be on leave again next week. This time I have decided to listen to my travel agent, and I won't be trying to cram too much in. Just a couple of bucket list visits this time around.

It will come as no surprise that I have been suffering from FOMO ever since my last trip, so I am extremely excited that the first destination on my itinerary will be the Laundry. I have been doing so much research and I cannot wait. In fact, I'm not exactly sure why I have never been there before.

Oh, and the good news is that I did call my therapist after my last diary entry, and she assured me that I am well liked. Must remember to tell my wife that.

Dear Diary,

Well, I am back from leave again, and would love nothing more than to tell you that I am well rested; but I am just frustrated, incredibly frustrated.

The *highlight* of my trip - my visit to the Laundry - was not all that it was cracked up to be. Or more precisely, it seems that I was researching the wrong Laundry altogether. You could imagine my disappointment when I discovered I had no reservation at The French Laundry in the Napa Valley. My Laundry had no river rock, no timber, no billowing white ceiling, and definitely no Thomas Keller-inspired classic dishes. My Laundry only had a washer, a dryer, a reverberating echo that caused migraines for days, and an incessant offensive stench inspired by my daughter's gym clothes.

The only excitement was that in the corner of my Laundry, I found a tiny door. It took me a while to pry it open, but I was both amazed and intrigued at what lay on the other side. Mystical like the Matterhorn, it was a Mountain. A mountain made up of socks. So I summoned my inner Sir Edmund Hillary, and with the help of a Sherpa who lives at the end of my street, I began to scale its heady heights. Upon closer inspection, there were no pairs of socks to be found. Just single garments, a kaleidoscope of multi-coloured material strewn aimlessly upon one another. I wonder what this all means?

More research for me then, but please do not fret. I have another appointment with my therapist booked in for this afternoon.

CHAPTER 2
MAY

Dear Diary,

I have been having some strange dreams lately. Nightmares, in fact. The kind that you wake up from in a cold sweat, trembling with fear. The type that leave you dizzy and disorientated, taking you a while to realise it was only an illusion.

I am not certain how these surfaced as I don't normally dream. In fact, I have been exercising more, eating (fairly) healthily and trying to meditate daily. The only thing I can put it down to is that I did watch a promo for *Tiger King*. Apart from making me physically ill, I am sure it left a psychological scar I will never, ever recover from.

In my dream I have just finished a week-long sales trip and am boarding QF746, an early evening flight back to Sydney from Adelaide. The flight is completely full. There's no room to slouch back in my chair and relax. I am a creature of habit so as I sit in my seat, ear phones go on, book comes out, and I try and ignore the outside world until we are just about to land.

I apparently arrived at the airport in a rush, straight from my last sales call, and I only just make my flight. Must remember to tell my assistant not to schedule my last meeting so close to my departure. Oh, that's right, I have no assistant.

No time, then, to enjoy the Lounge, which is normally where I would grab a drink and a bite to eat. So when I see the trolley rolling past, I take my earphones off.

'Dinner this evening?'

'What are the choices?' I ask, my inner English teacher silently admonishing myself that I answered a question with a question.

'Pasta...' Good start.

'... with mushrooms, ...' Nice.

'... bacon...' Bonus.

'... and cauliflower.' Silence.

Did I just hear 'cauliflower'?
Now, each to their own BUT how could you include such a divisive
vegetable in that combination?

'Is there an alternative?'

'Yes,' comes the quick reply. 'You can either choose to have it or not.'

With a look of disdain, disgust and defeat, I giggle through clenched
teeth as I slowly put my earphones back on.

I know it's autumn and cauliflowers are in season. I also appreciate
that this means it is readily available and most likely quite cost-
effective when working with a huge food budget. But what in the
hell was Neil Perry smoking when he put that menu together? Maybe
the bacon was supposed to disguise the taste of the cauliflower?
But what about that funk? Both in and out. Closed space. Captive
audience. What was he thinking???

Dear Diary,

I would love nothing more than to confide in you that my weird and wonderful dreams have ceased. To let you know that after the sun has well and truly set, I am able to lay my head down to sleep and I do not wake in a quivering heap.

Yet sadly, that is not the case, and my troubled mind still conjures eerie images that wake me violently from my slumber.

I am still no closer to grasping the genesis of these visions. But this week I am putting it down to TikTok, where once-aspiring Instagram models have turned into budding choreographers, elbow popping, dabbing, clapping, swinging, clicking, swaying, bouncing and twerking their way into our hearts. We should be grateful they only last 15 seconds. Is that the limit of their talent, or the limit of our attention spans in 2020? Whichever the case, their cultural contribution to society is irreversible.

In this dream it is 2011 and I am on a sales mission through India. It is February 25th, just before the heat becomes unbearable, especially for a suit-wearing, tie-sporting rep like me. Having just finished a week of calls in Mumbai, I have a few days to myself before flying to Delhi. I exit the Taj Mahal Palace Hotel, where I am staying, with a spring in

my step. I am excited, for my destination tonight is Leopold Café &
Bar, somewhere I have always wanted to visit, ever since I read the
book *Shantaram*. By the way, I am still not convinced about whether
the story is fiction or non-fiction, and the ongoing saga that is the
movie/TV adaptation is just as intriguing; Russell Crowe becomes
Johnny Depp becomes Charlie Hunnam. But I digress.

I actually take the long way around Colaba to my target, as I want
a closer look at the old Regal Cinema, an amazing art deco movie
theatre which was one of the first in the city to offer an elevator -
from the underground parking to the auditorium, no less. I finally
reach Leopold's, where the sign reads 'Since 1871', and head straight
past the café and up the stairs to the bar. It's Friday night, after all.
It is technically the weekend. The T20 World Cup is on. Groups Stage.
Australia vs NZ. And if that wasn't enough, it was my birthday earlier
in the week.

It's still relatively early by Indian standards, so I quickly find an empty
stool at the bar. Perfect. I have learnt that when travelling alone, a
barman is your best friend and just as important as your concierge.
So I sit right in front of the TV, between some fellow travellers, and
turn to my right with a cold Kingfisher in my hand.

Three Swedish super troupers await me, laughing and carrying
on. They proceed to tell me they live and work in Bandra. I hear
something about working for a charity and the dorms they live in, but
sadly that is where the conversation ends. I genuinely want to know
more of their Nordic tale but between them taking shots and drinking
beer, their mind/speech commands quickly become AWOL. Their
words are now incoherent as their undivided attention turns to the
coordinates of the latrine.

As I slowly turn away, I smile at the irony that their accents still
somehow remained charming.

On my left sits my new Iranian friend, who is quick to grab my
attention. She is alone and only too pleased to share her story with
someone other than the glass of bourbon that she cradles in her two
hands, akin to a priest holding a chalice prior to communion. She
explains that this is the last leg of her biannual trip throughout Asia,
already having visited Thailand and Indonesia. Her tale is fascinating

for she is a trader buying fabric to take back to Tehran, which she sells to friends and family from her apartment.

It is at that moment that I hear the unwanted roar from the TV above me. I turn rapidly and look up with dread and shock on my face. My jaw drops as the almost empty beer bottle slips from my hand, hitting the floor beneath me, and glass shatters all around. How could this be? This must be Fake News. NZ have just beaten the Baggy Greens.

PS. A quick check of the records will show Australia actually beat NZ on that fateful night by 7 wickets, but I have often been told that one should never let the truth get in the way of a good story.

Dear Diary,

In my role, I travel constantly for work. I am responsible for the Asia-Pacific region and I am away from home for at least one week every month, sometimes two. It is 'part of the job' and I have become accustomed to always being on the go.

So during these crazy times, I have come to realise how much I really, REALLY miss my trips, but perhaps not for the reasons you might think.

Of course, I miss the anticipation: confirming my flights and accommodation, sometimes a hire car, the scheduling of meetings, my visit to the Post Office to send a parcel addressed to myself, the packing of my suitcase the night prior to my departure making sure I have enough clothes to match how many days I am away.

Of course, I miss the trip itself: the early morning transfers to the airport, the Lounge access (oh, the Lounge access), the excitement of a boarding call (minus any delays), the flight (minus any turbulence), travelators, escalators, elevators, conveyor belts, a transfer to my 'home' for the duration of my stay.

Of course, I miss seeing my amazing clients: the wake-up calls, the traffic, the visits to their offices, the updates, the questions, the quotes, the bookings, the laughs, the issues, the stories of happy clients, the emails, and if I am lucky, seeing some of them for a drink and/or meal during the week.

But the main reason I miss not being able to travel is my pyjamas.

See, when I am at home, I have a system. I wear my PJs for three nights in a row before tossing them into the wash, then I wear a new pair for three nights, and so on and so on. It might surprise you that I don't have a pair for every day of the week. Amongst several reasons,

I just don't have the wardrobe space, as this is my wife's frontline. My clothes crossing those borders would constitute an act of aggression and war would be inevitable.

Apart from keeping the peace, I have found that my system allows me to keep my PJs looking (and smelling) wonderfully new and fresh.

My dilemma, though, is that I quite often forget how many days I have worn my PJs. Call it old age or absentmindedness, but whenever this occurred in the past, I had an easy formula to figure it out. I would simply count back to the day I arrived home. For instance, if I landed last Saturday night I knew it would be: Saturday, Sunday, Monday and change. Tuesday, Wednesday and bingo! I have another night before I need to swap again. Genius and foolproof.

Or so I thought, because now I am in a flux. I walk around all day in a haze of confusion, unable to concentrate at the task at hand. And if I am being completely honest, I fear night time the most, for that is when the real demons come out to play. I dread heading for my nightly shower because as soon as I bring out my PJs, the perspiration starts to trickle down my back. Has it been two nights or three already? I just can't remember!

I returned home from my last trip on Saturday 29th February. I can't count back that far. I can't even remember what I had for lunch last Wednesday. Hold on, what was that rhyme?

30 days hath September, April, June and November - they aren't even in order.

All the rest have 31, but February's 28 - no it doesn't, it has 29 because it's a leap year and the Olympics have been postponed!

I am just confused and I know my PJs are confused too. I hear them whispering when I wear them for only two nights before swapping them. 'What have we done to deserve this? I thought he loved us?'

And then again when I have worn a pair for four, maybe even five nights.

'Seriously? He's coming in again! Close the leg hole, close the leg hole!'

I so miss travelling. So do my pyjamas.

Dear Diary,

I once heard that the word *moist* was the most hated word in the English language. Hate is such a strong emotion and I for one am nonplussed with the vitriol. This particular word has done nothing to me apart from arming me with another adjective to express a certain moment in time. Like when I am in Singapore on business, how irritated I get between sales calls when I go from a super-airconditioned office out to the street below, and my glasses fog up and get all moist.

As you can tell, I enjoy both words and phrases. I love how they can express and communicate our feelings so succinctly. I get intrigued at their origin. Such as how some come into vogue after generations of hibernation whilst others appear into our vernacular out of nowhere like a Stone Cold Stunner or an RKO. I am also enthralled by the semantics of words and phrases. And how we can often draw different conclusions to their meaning when we decide to strip them bare and manipulate them in some way, shape or form.

Yet there are some words and phrases that irk me. In fact, there are currently three that I dislike more and more with each passing day:

1. **Travel Bubbles** - In this context, *bubble* is a *protected, exempt or unique area* and NOT a *spherical body of gas contained in a liquid* (here we go again with moist). So this is the chosen phrase to describe the short-term travel agreement between certain countries that have positively handled this crisis. I sort of get it, but the two things I instantly think of when I hear the word *bubble* are The Bubble Boy from Seinfeld and Bubble O'Bill ice creams. Both thoughts make me smile, and although I often travelled to the local milk bar for an ice cream, I am not sure this is what they are referring to. And don't get me started on the alternative of *Air Corridors*. I think I owned a pair of those when I used to play basketball.

2. **Fluid** - Not the noun and *being of liquid form* as we are not being moistened, doused and immersed under water (there it is again). In this context it is an adjective, as in: our situation is *changing readily; shifting; is not fixed, stable or rigid*. But isn't this true of EVERY situation? Life itself has always evolved and will continue to do so. So has the travel experience. Most rivers meander down a certain path but some can change and flow in the opposite direction. I bet you never realised river cruising would qualify as adventure travel? So in essence, the situation is not fluid; it is evolving and we are simply adapting in accordance with the knowledge we possess.

3. **The New Normal** - I have two issues with this particular phrase. *Normal* is something that is *regular; natural; serving to establish a standard*. Firstly, if you accept that the situation is fluid, then how do we know what the *new 'normal'* will be? We don't. So please stop feeding us with absurd assumptions and just state the facts. We are all trying to adapt to a way of life that balances our basic needs both medically and economically. There is nothing *new* about this. This has always been *normal*. Secondly, why do we need to use the word *new* in front of *normal*? Once something becomes a standard, doesn't it just become normal? And who defines what is and what isn't normal, anyway? Not that I cared, but while I was growing up I was often told that I didn't have a normal name. Then when a certain hotelier's daughter burst onto the scene, mine became an accepted moniker. I do owe her some gratitude, though, because in some strange way, her notoriety did validate my career choice!

Anyway, the situation remains fluid, and with all these travel bubbles, the new normal will be here faster than you realise.

CHAPTER 3
JUNE

123-456-789-101

Dear Diary,

I remember when *Back to the Future* was released in 1985 starring Michael J Fox and all the hype surrounding it. I actually went to the cinema to see all three movies in the franchise and argued for days with my friends as to whether III was better than II, or if they should have just walked away after the original. I also remember getting into heated discussions regarding all the futuristic gadgets on display and whether they were truly realistic or just a by-product of an overactive Hollywood imagination. I still find it fascinating that these movies included drones, voice command, smart home gadgets, augmented reality, smart glasses, tablets, finger print scanners, self-tying shoes, hover boards and even video calling.

Did someone say Zoom? Founded in 2011, *Zoom is the leader in modern enterprise video communications, with an easy, reliable cloud platform for video and audio conferencing, collaboration, chat, and webinars across mobile devices, desktops, telephones, and room systems.* There are so many conspiracy theories about the advent of COVD-19 but regardless of what their website states, I think we are all in agreement that Zoom was behind this pandemic.

I for one had never heard of or used Zoom prior to March this year. I can honestly say that the first thing that I thought of when someone mentioned Zoom, was the song by Fat Larry's Band. By the way, I first heard that little ditty on *Solid Gold*. You can find the song on Spotify and the film clip is on YouTube if you are intrigued to see how fat Fat Larry was.

Fast forward to June, and one could say I am now a Zoom expert of sorts. A savant, if you will. I use the platform almost daily, hosting several webinars every week, participating in many others, and even organising Saturday night drink sessions with friends.

The travel industry has always attracted colourful individuals so it would come as no surprise if I told you how smaller webinars resemble the opening/closing theme of *The Brady Bunch*, whilst larger webinars resemble the opening/closing theme of *The Muppet Show*.

But I also thought you might be interested in hearing about some observations that only a Zoom Master (tenth degree Black Belt, no less) would be able to notice about Zoom participants. For example, there is always:

> One who enters your personal meeting room way too early - *I kind of feel violated, to be honest, and need to shower afterwards.*

> One who is always late - *No real harm done unless that person is the host.*

> One whose video never works and is a constant black screen - *I find it extremely unnerving and difficult to concentrate when this occurs. I just keep wondering what they are really doing/ wearing. OK, sorry, back to the meeting.*

> One whose audio never works and who types all their questions in the chat - *Should we just email each other? A phone call, perhaps?*

> One wearing a headset - *Please drive through to the next window to pick up your order.*

> One who attempts to send a private message but sends it to everyone - *The equivalent to a Reply All email fail.*

> One who forgets to mute themselves - *The constant background noise causing them to flicker ominously like a neon sign in a film noir.*

> One who comes dressed to the nines - *I'm a model, you know what I mean, and I do a little turn on the catwalk.*

> One who is continuously changing their virtual background - *Guilty as charged.*

One intrigued by this, who asks for step-by-step instructions to do the same - *There goes the next 10 minutes.*

One who's chosen the wrong virtual background and now looks like they are the host of the *Mulligrubs* – *If you know, you know.*

One eating or drinking (or both) - *Ooh that looks good! Wonder where they got that from?*

One who keeps looking off into the distance (right, left, behind them) – *So glad I am not boring you.*

One who keeps talking over everyone – *Wonder if there is a button that plays 'wrap it up' music like at the Oscars?*

One whose pet randomly walks in front of their camera – *I jumped in fright the first time this happened.*

Dear Diary,

I work for an amazing company that both values and respects its employees. I like to think that I am good at my job and that I have forged a fairly successful career in my chosen field. I know what I do is not life changing, but you could say that I was always destined to work in sales.

Growing up, I was like most teenagers and had posters up on my wall. With the perfect amount of Blu Tack on each corner (my mother was definitely not afraid to take off her slipper and 'use it' on me if I damaged the wallpaper), up went the flavour of the month. I went through many phases and the likes of Prince, Cindy Crawford and Bruce Lee graced the bedroom which I shared with my older brother. But the one poster that always remained up was the one of Tim Shaw.

For those who don't remember or don't know, Tim Shaw was the Demtel Man back in the 1990s. Demtel popularised infomercials with their 'As Seen On TV' ads which predated the shopping channel phenomenon. Interestingly, we still have TVSN in Australia; although I am certain that in our capitalist society, online shopping has surpassed TV shopping as the preferred choice in a free market economy. Go figure. Tim became famous because of his smile. He was also loud, garish, relentless and a pain in the butt, all whilst offering viewers a set of steak knives with any purchase of the product he was spruiking, but only if it was bought within a certain time frame. What was not to admire?

So why am I opening up my soul for all to see, and telling you about my childhood idol? Well, MMXX is just like an infomercial, but of the worst kind - written by Stephen King, directed by Quentin Tarantino, starring Kim Kardashian and Steven Segal, costumes and musical score by Helen Keller. You get the idea. And just when you think things could not get any worse, Tim Shaw utters those four hypnotising words: 'But wait, there's more!'

Someone a lot wiser than me once said, 'Those who do not remember the past, are condemned to repeat it.' And if you take a look at every grim event that has occurred since January 1st, it paints a very bleak picture indeed: bushfires in Australia, floods in Indonesia, the assassination of an Iranian General by a drone which directly led to a Ukrainian passenger jet being shot down in retaliation, earthquakes in Turkey and the Caribbean, a volcanic eruption in the Philippines, a plague of locusts in East Africa, riots in Delhi, a mass shooting in a Thailand mall, too many mass shootings in the US to name individually, a gas plant explosion in Nigeria, the murder of George Floyd and subsequent protests and, of course, COVID-19 being declared a pandemic.

But I am also reminded that Martin Luther King Jr said: 'We are not makers of history. We are made by history.' So just as the events above are sobering reminders that we are not makers of history, the events below remind us that we are indeed made by history:

Brexit. *Yes, it finally happened. I am just glad that a decision was reached one way or the other. All this on again, off again, on again talk was exhausting, infuriating and above all damaging to the UK economy. Interestingly, also COMPLETELY similar to the ongoing saga of a proposed Spice Girls Reunion.*

Impeachment Trial of Donald Trump. *You're fired!*

Acquittal of Donald Trump. *OK, maybe not.*

Duke and Duchess of Sussex Stepping Down from Royal Duties. *So let me get this straight. Harry and Meaghan left home after getting married, to become financially independent? Harry is 35yo. Meaghan is 38yo. About time Charles kicked them out and told them to get proper jobs. Now maybe he and Camilla can become true empty nesters and start cruising on the QE2 full-time.*

Tokyo Olympics Postponed. *Did you know that the organisers of the 2020 Winter Olympics gave out 110,000 condoms? In Rio in 2016, the average was 42 condoms per athlete. For a two-*

week event. As hard as it may be, forget about the obvious for a moment. Latex in this form is non-biodegradable. Can you imagine how much we just saved the environment? The fish must be celebrating by doing triple-somersault inward dives in the tuck position. Speaking of fish...

Trikinis. *Really? I mean, really? These are now a thing? Not to be pedantic, but where is the male equivalent? And what do you call a male version anyway? You can't call it a bikini, that's already taken and would be confusing. The mask could come in handy for fishing, though. I find there are only so many sardines one can stuff down one's Speedos. I have spent way too much time and energy thinking about this, haven't I?*

Murder Hornets in the US. *You couldn't make this stuff up if you tried, could you? In basic terms, they are just really (really) big wasps that come from Asia and look a little different from regular ones, especially in terms of colour. Why does that sound familiar? Anyway, if you thought they were bad, just wait until the invasion of the Drop Bears and Exploding Unicorns.*

Eurovison Song Contest Cancelled. *Forget about the Olympics - this is the real travesty! I for one will miss seeing the entire legitimate and non-partisan voting process. This was, after all, the contest that helped launch the careers of Cliff Richard, ABBA, Julio Iglesias, Celine Dion (did you know she was Swiss? No, neither did I). And to think that Australia had a realistic chance of winning. Yes. Australia. That island nation just off the coast of Portugal.*

Dear Diary,

The nightmares have returned.

I thought I had rid myself of these horrible visions but last night they came back with a vengeance. They ambushed me like a runaway freight train, chasing me relentlessly down the tracks until they extinguished my very being.

And as I lay awake in my bed in the dead of night trying to rock myself back to sleep, chest heaving, limbs trembling, I tried once more to decipher from whence these illusions had emerged.

Perhaps it was news that a *Friends* reboot was on its way. The hype of a soon-to-be reunion raising our expectations, yielding unrealistic promises until we are ultimately left deflated and disappointed. Not all recycled goods are useful, and just like a one-legged man in a kicking contest, I am certain this re*boot* will fall flat on its face. Then again, for $2.5 million, *I'll be there for you* anytime you'd want me to.

So in this dream it is June 17th, 2014 and I find myself in South Korea on business. Probably the most annoying aspect of travelling so much is that you inevitably miss out on important milestones like birthdays, anniversaries, weddings and State of Origin.

See, in Game 1 of this year, NSW held on to beat QLD 12-8 up in Brisbane. Game 2 is scheduled to be played the day after I land in Seoul. It will be in Sydney, which means the Blues have a realistic chance of winning the match and series, their first in 9 years. Yes, sadly the Maroons have won 8 series in a row. I still feel ill saying that out loud - like when you try and lick a cane toad for a quick high, and the outcome is immediately regretted.

I love Seoul. There is a language barrier, of course, but you can get by with some perseverance and resourcefulness. Catching taxis is an interesting sport. New York City cab drivers might have the reputation, but the ones in Korea are the craziest. It always feels like jumping on a roller-coaster when you enter their vehicle; you must strap yourself in, ensuring the roll bar is pulled down and locked in place.

I am staying at The Plaza at City Hall and once I am checked in, a search on Google provides me with the phone number of Tony's Aussie Bar and Bistro. I am a man on a mission so I call up and speak to Tony himself:

'Hi. Do you have a TV screen?

'Yes,' comes the monotone reply.

'Do you play live sporting events from Australia?'

'Yes.' Almost there.

'Will you be showing the State of Origin tomorrow night?'

'Yes.' We have lift off!

A quick calculation of the time difference divided by the kick-off time equals: I need to be there by 7pm.

'Great, I will see you at 7pm.'

'That's the time we open, so make sure you grab something to eat before you get here because we don't serve food.'

Silence from my end as confusion ensues.

Have I really just found the Pub With No Beer?

He did say this was Tony's Aussie Bar and *Bistro*, right?

If they don't serve food, shouldn't it just be Tony's Aussie *Bar*?

Truth be told, I normally try to avoid Australian pubs when I am overseas. I just don't get the point of travelling to a foreign country only to seek out a watering hole that reminds me of the ones back home. Instead, I would much rather immerse myself in the culture of the particular country that I find myself in. For me, that almost always means finding local restaurants. In Korea I love the *Buchimgae*, and of course, Korean BBQ. I have been fortunate enough to have been taken to some amazing Korean BBQ joints that I would never have found on my own. And I can proudly say I am a Jeju

pork convert, and I rate it as some of the best on the planet. I am still unsure about *Naengmyeon* but as they say, when in Seoul...

So no Australian pubs for me unless there is an important sporting event being played. I know what you are thinking: this statement is truly oxymoronic as ALL sporting events are important. You are correct. The added bonus here is that 2014 is also a World Cup year and it will be Australia vs Holland right after the State of Origin. So Tony's it is then!

The bar is located in Itaewon, which is Seoul's international district, right next to the American Army barracks. There is a seedy side to the area but that is thankfully on the other side of the main road. On this side there are only many (many) bars, some very cool restaurants and Tony's Aussie Bar and Bistro. Tony is a character and drummer of some note, and has his drum kit and studio downstairs.

Sadly, Tony's no longer exists. He sold up and moved back to Australia. Thankfully I have some good memories of it, and also made some great friends there whom I still keep in touch with on my travels.

And if you are wondering, NSW beat QLD 6-4 in a very dour, defensive match, to win the series. Australia would unfortunately lose 2-3 to Holland in one of the best games of the tournament. That Timmy Cahill goal was a screamer, though; an absolute stunner straight from the top drawer. It still gives me chills just thinking about it. And I definitely had to eat before I got to Tony's Aussie Bar minus the Bistro.

PS. My earlier mention of cane toads was not a random one. We love nicknames in Australia and for some unknown reason during State of Origin, New South Welshmen are lovingly referred to as Cockroaches and Queenslanders as Cane Toads.

Dear Diary,

When I was younger, I used to sleep walk. I was a source of constant amusement for family and friends, who would marvel at the fact that the morning after, I could not remember one damn thing that I got up to the night before.

When I was growing up in the Blue Mountains west of Sydney, my parents owned their own business, which meant they worked extremely long hours, 7 days a week. As a result, any entertaining would occur late at night once they were well and truly home.

Being the youngest of three children, my bedtime was the earliest so I would invariably say goodnight before anyone had arrived. I don't know if I was showing early signs of my FOMO addiction or just had a curious adolescent's mind, but this is when my nocturnal escapades began.

The most common occurrence would be me getting up from my bed, heading out to the living room and like a good host, engaging with whomever was around - uncles, aunts, cousins, family friends, I never discriminated. I would sit down with our guests, join their conversations and sample the cheese and fruit on offer plus maybe a cheeky glass of H_2O before heading back to bed. The following morning, I always knew when I had been the life of the party because my brother and sister would be giggling hysterically before telling me of my antics.

On many other occasions I would apparently stand up in my bed in the dead of night, look up at the poster on my wall (sadly not the one of Cindy Crawford which I mentioned previously - that would come several years later) and shout, 'Pass it! Pass it!' to Slippery Steve Morris, the St George Dragons Halfback who was holding a rugby league ball in the photo.

There was also the infamous time when two of my cousins slept over. They were around my older brother's age and I was the first to have to go to bed. So there I was on the top bunk fast asleep, my brother on the bottom bunk and my two cousins on mattresses adjacent. They had stayed up to all hours chatting about whatever teenage boys talked about. And just as they finally nodded off to sleep, a deafening thud echoed through the entire house followed by screams of horror.

It woke everyone up and as they rushed in and turned on our bedroom light, there I was, lying on top of one of my cousins, his arms and legs flailing in the air under me, and he was yelling, 'GET HIM OFF ME!' as loud as he could muster.

I had apparently fallen from my top bunk and *splat!* landed right on top of him. Thankfully, he was there to break my fall with his face, but I don't think he saw it that way. And yet I never woke up. I just calmly climbed back up to my bed, covered myself with my blanket and went back to sleep. The next morning, I didn't remember a thing, although I did have an impressive bruise on my leg because I had also hit my brother's stereo on my way down.

I still don't remember much about my sleepwalking except from one vivid memory, a recurring vision in which I could float through the air. I could levitate up from my bed and to the other side of the room. Sometimes, I would even head out the front door and float down the street, perhaps somewhat similar to that boy floating outside the window in *Salem's Lot*. And if you remember the original version, then you'll have chills just reading this.

So why am I sharing more childhood memories with you? Perhaps it's because I feel that I have come full circle. *Déjà vu* almost. Growing up, I obviously dreamt in my sleep about flying and travelling, even if it was just to the other side of my bedroom. Up until very recently, some would say that I was living the dream being able to fly and travel on a regular basis. Yet ever since March, I find myself walking in a constant daze, daydreaming about flying and travelling once more.

CHAPTER 4
JULY
№ 123-456-789-009

Dear Diary,

Anyone that knows me well, or anybody who lurks in the shadows of my social media accounts, may have realised that I am a sucker for professional wrestling.

And like many who will read this, my wife thinks I am nuts.

I originally got hooked because of my father. As an impressionable young lad, I loved hearing him regale us with tales of being at the old Sydney Stadium or White City, to watch Australian wrestlers like Roy Heffernan, Larry O'Dea and Ron Miller fight international stars like Brute Bernard, Mark Lewin, Killer Kowalski, Tex McKenzie, Mario Milano and Spiros Arion.

Wrestling was so popular in Australia that from 1964-1978 there was even a locally produced, weekly TV show called *World Championship Wrestling*. Jack Little was the original host but at some stage Michael Cleary came onto the scene. If that name sounds vaguely familiar, it is because he is one of only four Aussies to represent his country in three different sports. His time in wrestling, dealing with all the drama and larger than life characters, must have also honed his arbitrary and moderating skills too, because he became a politician and was even the NSW State Minister for Sports, Recreation and Tourism for several years.

One of the fondest memories that I have with my dad, was in the mid-80s when he got us tickets to the Sydney Entertainment Centre to watch a WWF live event. That's the World Wrestling Federation, now known as WWE, and not to be confused with the World Wildlife Fund, now known as World Wide Fund for Nature, as that would just be weird.

Seeing the likes of Ricky 'The Dragon' Steamboat, The Magnificent Muraco, The Iron Sheik and George 'The Animal' Steele was a dream come true for this young fan.

And now that I am a responsible parent, I have done my fatherly duty and passed on my love for the sport to my daughter.

Sneer if you must, but there are many reasons to admire wrestling: it is an escape from reality; the wrestlers themselves are outrageously athletic and insanely talented; it's incredibly entertaining; the story lines are about as believable as one would normally find in soap operas; the acting is WAY better.

Wrestling is big business and there is a long list of performers who have become successful actors. For instance, did you know that Oddjob in James Bond's *Dr No* was played by Harold Sakata, otherwise known as Tosh Togo? Or that mafia boss Luca Brasi in *The Godfather* was ex-wrestler Lenny Montana? Other wrestlers that made names for themselves in Hollywood include Andre The Giant (*The Princess Bride*), Rowdy Roddy Piper (*They Live*), Dave Bautista (*Guardians of the Galaxy*), and John Cena (*Trainwreck*).

But without a doubt, the most famous crossover star has to be Dwayne 'The Rock' Johnson. Today, The Rock is so well known and respected as an actor, that it is entirely possible you might know him more for his list of film credits than his wrestling days. Yet in the beginning he was a third-generation superstar who was 'without a doubt the most electrifying man in sports entertainment'; and if you don't believe that he would personally 'take you down to Know Your Role Boulevard, which is on the corner of Jabroni Drive, and check you directly into the Smackdown Hotel!'

Dear Diary,

I am sure you will agree that during this very peculiar year, many have taken the time to re-evaluate their lives. And while we have been left gazing into the abyss, we have also been gifted an opportunity to reconsider what is really important to us.

I too have been reflecting deeply and have had some revelations of my own. I would therefore like to propose some changes in the way society perceives 'value' and 'worth' and how 'precious' certain commodities really are.

As we head into July, I am reminded that in just a few short weeks, had all been well, the Olympic flame for the Games of the XXXII Olympiad would have been burning brightly.

I feel for the athletes. Imagine training for four years, only to have the opportunity of competing on the greatest stage of them all taken away from you by something beyond your control. Imagine the dedication and sacrifices they have made. Imagine the blood, sweat and tears that they have shed. All for nothing.

While Tokyo is postponed, I would like us to all reconsider the rewards currently given to these athletes, for they are outdated and do not accurately reflect their eternal effort:

3rd Place - Bronze Medal

Bronze is an alloy that is made of copper plus at least one other metal, usually tin. It was the first compound ever made and was incredibly useful and versatile. When it was mixed with zinc, we even crafted coins from it for our monetary systems. For these reasons, bronze was seen as extremely valuable since the beginning of time. Yet it also became apparent that too much exposure to the elements caused bronze disease. The Bronze Age did last for 1800 years but it has now lost its patina. Even bronzed bodies have become passé. In today's society, a very generous estimate has Bronze worth AUD $0.01/gram.

I therefore propose we ditch Bronze Medals and give every third placed athlete a Kardashian. I am certain there are enough of them to go around and, similar to bronze, they are not very appealing or useful on their own. They are also ductile, can cause disease if given too much exposure and, most importantly, do not produce sparks when struck. The obligatory podium photos will look amazing, yet they will be invariably thrown to the bottom of the drawer and forgotten about.

2nd Place - Silver Medal

Silver is a soft, lustrous, precious metal valued for its decorative beauty and electrical conductivity. My concern is that silver is so adaptable that is has lost its value and sells at only AUD $0.83/gram. Consider how common it has become, for it is literally everywhere. Every cloud now has a silver lining. Not a few, or some, but EVERY cloud. Every minute, countless children are being born with a silver spoon in their mouth, and all manner of things are handed out willy-nilly on silver platters. No wonder Long John Silver never found his treasure. Everyone else had it.

So my suggestion is that every runner-up receives a roll of Toilet Paper. Firstly, let me be clear, there is no truth to the rumour that I am just bitter because I somehow missed my chance at becoming a silver fox. Like silver, toilet paper is soft, antimicrobial and non-toxic. It is also quite valuable; just ask anyone who went out shopping for essentials at the beginning of the pandemic. I don't believe it conducts electricity, although I do know I feel a positive surge whenever I reach for some. And just like in folklore, toilet paper also has mystical powers depending on whether you fold, crumple or wrap. The only negative is that, similar to silver, it too can be tarnished. In fact, I guarantee you it will be tarnished.

1st Place - Gold Medal

Gold is the earliest recorded element employed by humans and is unique because it's a transition metal. It is resistant to corrosion and is both a thermal and electrical conductor. Most importantly, it is dense, durable, malleable, pure and extremely attractive. Yet although it sells at an impressive AUD $83.36/gram, I fear it is no longer as scarce as it once was. For instance, many receive a golden handshake when they reach the golden age, so they can enjoy their golden years with their Golden Girls (am I the only one who sees the irony that they were never on the silver screen?). There are also many tales of gold diggers ending up with fool's gold because they forgot the golden rule that all that glitters is NOT gold. Someone should really remind them that the pot of gold is at the end of the rainbow, never under the golden arches. Silence is still golden, but having a heart of gold is now seen as a weakness. Oh, the gilt!

Gold was once a symbol of wealth, prosperity and success. So we need something just as rare, precious and alluring. The perfect reward for victory must be an airline Boarding Pass. A Golden Ticket, if you will. Like Charlie Bucket scoffing down a Wonka Bar and finding his ultimate prize, it would be life changing. 007 defeated foes with a Goldfinger, a GoldenEye, and a Golden Gun; so true champions deserve a boarding pass, for they are unique and can also Bond with other elements - airport lounges, aeroplanes, transfers, hotels.

As the son of a Greek immigrant, I believe I have the responsibility and authority to make such changes. And I hope that with your backing, we can get the IOC to agree. The athletes are depending on us.

Dear Diary,

I have worked in Hospitality for over 25 years. Before losing my soul to sales, I also was a room service attendant, in charge of the mini-bar trolley, a waiter, a barman and a banquets coordinator.

My first luxury hotel sales role was with The Windsor in Melbourne, which at that time was owned and managed by Oberoi. The Windsor was built in 1883, is rightfully heritage listed, and is Victorian in both style and location. It was fondly dubbed the *Duchess of Spring Street* and in its time it was THE place to stay in town. One of its most infamous guests was racing car driver-come-socialite 'Captain' Peter Janson, who lived at the hotel for over a decade. His escapades are legendary, his parties were fabulously notorious, and he is often credited for turning the Melbourne Cup into the carnival it is today.

Although I was only a Sales Executive at the time, I used to look after the KPMG account, which was an important one for the hotel. In fact, I can clearly remember the day I was invited in to meet their newly appointed Travel Manager. I remember it vividly because I also needed to discuss the upcoming contract renewal process with them.

Their office was located around the corner from the hotel at the aptly named Paris End of Collins Street. So at 9.50am, I exited our office for our 10am meeting. At 9.55am I entered the KPMG Building and was met at reception by Security.

'Can I help you?'

'Yes. I have a meeting with the new Travel Manager, France.'

'And your name?'

'Parris.'

No words. Just a perplexed look interspersed with the sound of butterflies flapping their wings in the distance.

'Sorry. Did you say your name is Parris?'

'Yes.'

'And you are here to meet France?'

'Yes.'

A smile crept across his lips. I think he even giggled. I definitely rolled my eyes.

'OK, then. I will just let her know that you are here.'

He was grinning now as he dialled her number.

'France, Parris is here to see you,' followed by hysterical laughter.

This could go on forever.

Who's on first? I don't know. Level 3!

It was a very successful meeting and as you might expect, Parris and France got on famously. France even confided in me how her parents named her France because they had first met in Paris. I remember thinking what a cute story that was, but how easily it could have been a disaster. Imagine if they had met in Istanbul?

Oh, the hotel ended up on the KPMG preferred list for another year. And I always had a chuckle with Security whenever I visited their office.

Dear Diary,

Like most of us, I have spent an inordinate amount of time at home during these last four months. The struggle is real and I too have felt the pressure to use my time wisely, be productive and become a better me.

The lockdown fads came thick and fast but thankfully I ignored most of them. The only exception is that I was able to add some new recipes to my culinary repertoire. I am definitely no handyman but I even tried my hand at vanquishing those pesky little jobs around the house that never seem to go away.

So if I am honest, I would say that I have spent most of my time at home catching up on the movies, documentaries and TV shows that I had always planned to watch but never had the time to do so.

Anyone who follows my drivel on social media knows that I often write movie reviews on Facebook. And up until very recently, the only time I really got to watch them was on an aeroplane flying to, or back from, a destination. During my homestay, Netflix has been indispensable and supplied me some good, some bad and some very ugly. Even Foxtel came to the party and offered free access to all their channels for 3 months. A great marketing strategy by them, especially as they have lost both their appeal and market share over the last several years.

I remember when I first subscribed to Foxtel back in 2005. I recall it clearly because I sat down with my very pregnant wife to make a deal with her. If she allowed me to get Foxtel, I would look after the graveyard shift from midnight to 6am when the baby arrived. My rationale was that she would get some rest and I would be able to watch all the live sporting events that would be shown overnight while bonding with our newborn and explaining which team(s) to support and why. So we signed our very own blood oath, sealed it with a kiss, and were blessed when a beautiful, healthy Pay TV service was delivered into our lives.

And for the first three months, it was the deal of a lifetime for my wife. But then our daughter turned a quarter of a year old and decided that she wanted to sleep right through from around 10pm to 6am. I distinctly remember the first time this occurred, and attempting to wake her up for her 3-hourly feed (our daughter, not my wife) but she wouldn't budge. She was having none of it and I became quite agitated because I had read all the books and listened to all the experts, and I knew that she needed another bottle. Being a novice parent, I actually got so distressed that I woke up my wife to tell her of the crisis at hand. With me all flustered and my wife half asleep, we called the early parenting service helpline to find out what we were doing wrong. The nurse we spoke to was just as shocked as we were. Shocked at our lack of lucidity. She laughed then chastised us, explaining that most parents call on the verge of a nervous breakdown desperately needing to find out how to put their baby to sleep - NOT to ask how to wake one up. We were strongly advised to just leave her be and say a little prayer that this pattern continued. If she was hungry and needed to be fed (again, our daughter not my wife), she would definitely let us know.

My daughter continued to sleep right through, although I now know that this is not the norm. I have heard some horror stories from many of our friends. One father I know even resorted to sleeping on the couch until their child turned 4 years old because they could never get them to sleep more than 2-3 hours at a time. And just when he made a triumphant return to his own bed, they decided to have another child and it was back to the couch for him.

I am now the proud father of a 15yo teenage girl who is strong, sassy, emotional, smart and funny. She supports all the right teams and still LOVES her sleep. And I still have my Foxtel.

Dear Diary,

I attended university and studied philosophy as part of the curriculum for my degree. Possessing a fairly curious mind, I had already read some Socrates, Plato and Aristotle, so I became bewitched with studying the likes of Rousseau, Marx and Nietzsche.

I never agreed with all their theories but it did instil in me the importance of keeping an open mind and questioning ideals. I learnt that one should never just accept the status quo and that there is nothing wrong with challenging the establishment. The arrogance of youth, after all, is a rite of passage which has often been the catalyst for change.

One theory that left a lasting impression on me was the belief that there is not just one Truth but instead, many truths. Truth be told, I can't even remember who conceptualised that (it might have been Camus), but I believe in it earnestly.

We are seeing it now in the Black Lives Matter movement and the realisation (finally) that history taught from just one perspective leads to injustice, whether deliberate or unintentional.

We are seeing it during this pandemic, whether it be debates on the origin of the virus and how to prevent contracting it, or between healthcare professionals and economists on what restrictions we should be enforcing.

And we are seeing it in the media portrayal of the travel industry, where emotional responses are coveted over facts. In their distorted reality, information has become collateral damage, and all that really matters are clickbait headlines and soundbites. They care not about the time and energy that travel agents have spent helping the masses get refunds and credits, battling around the clock with suppliers and operators. They do not report on the emotional distress and the financial losses they have suffered, because this does help them complete the Truth they are peddling.

I am also reminded that I too have lived this injustice where perception becomes reality. It was when I was a teenager and my brother was dating his now wife. Her parents had a holiday house up the coast, just 90 minutes north of Sydney at The Entrance. It was summer and I tagged along when he decided to drive up and stay for the week.

His girlfriend had a sister, so one evening the four of us decided to go ten pin bowling. With multiple games booked in advance, we were on our way when the girls remembered that they had forgotten to bring socks. We made a quick pit stop at the chemist but all they could find were some ankle high, single leg stockings.

It turned out that they had wasted their money because once we arrived, we discovered the bowling centre supplied spare socks to accessorise with those funky clown shoes they make you wear. As our impersonation of the Flintstones and Rubbles came to an end, we decided to pick up some pizzas for dinner on our way home. There were no Brontosaurus Burger joints around so we stopped off at a local Pizza Hut and the girls went in to order while my brother and I stayed in his car, in the carpark. Sometime between when they closed the car door, and when they came back with the pizzas, we had the ingenious idea of putting the recently bought nylons to good use. We decided it would be hilarious to cover our faces with them while we waited. We got a few strange looks from passers-by but when the girls returned with pizzas in hand, they howled with laughter. Mission accomplished.

When we arrived at the house, their parents frantically informed us that our parents had called from Sydney worried to death that we had been in some sort of accident. My brother immediately called my father to let him know we were fine. Dad mentioned that a Constable from The Entrance had called him about 30 minutes ago regarding the accident we had apparently been in. So my brother called the local police to let them know we were fine and this must have been a case of mistaken identity. But before he could do any of that, he was asked to come into the station to answer some questions.

Once there, I was petrified, confused and more than a little concerned. The Constable told us that apparently those strange looks we got waiting in the carpark were more than just that. The passers-by had called 000 and alerted the authorities about an armed robbery that was in progress at Pizza Hut. We were also told that we were extremely lucky as several police cars arrived at the scene just minutes after we must have left, oblivious to the scene unfolding behind us. They had the licence plate of the getaway car (which was registered in Sydney), hence the phone call to our parents. And somewhere in between, they all partook in a strange version of Chinese whispers, which changed the information from an armed robbery to a car accident.

So as you can see, it is easy for the facts to get distorted, depending on someone's point of view. Perhaps that is why I have always tried to look for reputable sources when reading my news. It becomes a chore, and not even *The Betoota Advocate* carries its weight anymore.

PS. I don't know how bank robbers do their job, because take it from me, wearing nylons over your face is extremely uncomfortable.

CHAPTER 5
AUGUST

Dear Diary,

In 2007 I hosted a trip to the US and drove a group of travel agents between Los Angeles and San Francisco in a minivan. It was a memorable work trip because I felt a little like Cliff Richard in the movie *Summer Holiday* minus the musical numbers and (as far as I am aware) police hunt.

The trip ended in San Francisco, where I took the opportunity to hire a convertible to drive back to Los Angeles via California Highway 1. It was the end of summer and the sun was shining, so the top came down and the wind felt exhilarating racing through my hair (it's my diary entry and I can write anything I want to).

It's an astonishing winding road of jagged coastline that juts and twists, revealing nature's true beauty on every turn. I remember making pit stops at Santa Cruz, Monterey and Carmel. Clint Eastwood was no longer Mayor but I was feeling lucky and it did make my day. The Big Sur is stunning, and I also recall a little café near the town of Lucia which had the most breathtaking views of the vista that one could ever wish for.

I stayed overnight in San Simeon, which is technically halfway between San Francisco and Los Angeles. At first glance, San Simeon is pretty much nondescript and could quite easily be from another dimension. I ended up in a motel along the highway and it was only the next day that I discovered the quaint little village of Cambria. It is so very pretty, and it is where I spent my afternoon with some locals in a bar, watching the Steelers play.

The main reason for staying in San Simeon was to visit Hearst Castle. This was the dream home of media mogul William Randolph Hearst, who was the real Rosebud and the inspiration for the Orson Welles classic *Citizen Kane*. Driving inland, the castle appears seemingly out of nowhere and took almost 30 years to build. Walking through his Xanadu, you can almost hear the music and laughter from the debauched and ostentatious parties held there. It is intimidating, beautiful, stunning and sad all at once. It even inspired me to write the following poem:

Her Castle

I have danced barefoot
Under the blazing moonlight
On a secluded island
Beside the Rich and Famous.

I have slumbered peacefully
Within lavish quarters
In an extravagant palace
Amongst Kings and Queens.

Yet your castle
On top of
The enchanted hill
Is the most amazing
Retreat
From reality
That I have ever
Gazed upon.

So, like Rapunzel,
Please let down
Your hair
So I can
Climb
Once more
To the top
Of your sanctuary.

As for all
The pleasures
I have savoured,
I would trade them
In a heartbeat
To spend
Just one night
With you.

My final destination on my road trip to Los Angeles was the timeless estate that is Hotel Bel-Air. Destiny is a curious beast, as it seems that I have always had a love affair with this hotel. How could you not, as you walk across that Brigadoon bridge to discover your own hidden sanctuary?

Dear Diary,

This week has been nondescript and exhilarating all at once. Let me explain.

Since March, I have felt utterly exhausted just standing idle. I have been doing my best John Cleese impression of being on a slow-moving travelator on a road to nowhere, heading in the opposite direction to my departure gate.

As a result, my mind has wandered aimlessly within the abyss that is my consciousness, and I have pondered over immaterial matters.

Like, why would a person choose to jog on the street amongst moving vehicles rather than on a much (much) safer footpath? Do these people not realise how dangerous this can be, especially when moving blindly with the traffic instead of against it? First we had cyclists to worry about (apologies to my lycra-wearing brethren), and now we have to dodge sweaty civilians with earphones tickling their tympanic cavities playing human Frogger. This is sadly a very common occurrence in my neighbourhood and I just don't get the logic. Oh, I get that on my street, one side of the road is paved whilst the other is just grass. I also get that it sometimes rains. But I would rather a soggy sneaker than a broken pelvis. You would think they would just cross the road to the other side, wouldn't you? I have never been a keen jogger, so I wonder if perhaps there is a science that suggests that with each stride exerting heel shock which is 3½ times your own body weight, it is best for one's foot to meet the hard, unforgiving asphalt rather than the soft, spongy turf below.

Or, how I am now 47 years old and losing my footing is no longer just 'falling over', but rather, is now described as 'having a fall'. I love my age. I don't feel old. I don't even feel middle-aged. I have plenty left to give and I have plenty still to learn. I really do feel like

I am just entering the prime of my life. Yet I am now apparently at that age where, whenever I open my Hotmail account, my Inbox is filled with messages about Viagra, Bitcoin, Russian dating sites and hemp gummies. Google Analytics must think I am either the head of a suburban crime syndicate or a writer of scripts for reality TV shows.

Or, even how up until very recently, I never knew there was a *Shrek 5* conspiracy theory. A quick check on the ever reliable, factual and newsworthy Wikipedia shows there is no *Shrek 5* listed. Yet there is an official teaser trailer for the movie. *Shrek 5* also has an official Twitter page, which apparently had a clock counting backwards to its release date in 2020, but which mysteriously disappeared. But if you visit IMDb, *Shrek 5* has a release date of 2022. What are they trying to hide? And who are they anyway? Some blame COVID-19. The pandemic has caused the cancellation of travel plans and the Olympics, and now it is robbing us of our favourite green ogre. I am referring to Shrek, of course, and not Elton John whenever he sees Madonna lip synching into the room. Some blame 5G because we can, and it is *Shrek 5* after all. Genius. Perhaps the conspiracy theorists figured out that we were all going to be microchipped via the popcorn and choc tops? Some even blame Donald Trump because he did, after all, promise to drain the swamp. Maybe he is the real-life Lord Farquaad?

On the flipside, on Wednesday I put on a suit for the very first time in months, and visited some clients. Yes. Real meetings with real people. I met one person for coffee and I visited another in their office. I felt all giddy and not just because I still fit into my trousers. Well, that was a major part of it. I was so excited I literally did the Tom Cruise thing. Just to clarify, that was the *Risky Business* sliding across the floor in my socks, underwear and shirt thing, not the Oprah disturbingly jumping up and down on the lounge and creeping everyone out thing. I was even able to put on my new cufflinks which had been sitting patiently in my top drawer since March. It felt like my first day back at work after being on holiday for a month.

In the immortal words of Ice Cube, Wednesday was a good day and I plan to make it a habit.

Dear Diary,

As I mentioned last week, I have started visiting clients again for coffee or, if they prefer, in their office. It has been invigorating and great for the mind, body and soul.

Because I have started wearing a suit again, I finally had some shirts to drop off at my local dry cleaner, whom I have not seen since March. They have been doing it tough and my heart goes out to all small businesses during this time. Like the semi-retired Englishman who lives in the suburb adjacent to mine, whom I use for my transfers to and from the airport. We always have a great yarn when he picks me up and he regales me with tales of when he used to work on the ships. I haven't seen him since February.

The Government must also be feeling the pinch because they can't collect their Passenger Movement Charge, or Departure Tax for short. And what about the fees they charge to renew your passport? Mine is still valid for a few more years, but I can't see many people rushing out to renew theirs at the moment even if they have expired.

In 2004 we embarked on a grandiose road trip across the North East of the US. The plan was New York City to Boston to Lenox to Manchester Village to Niagara Falls to Pittsburgh to Philadelphia.

New York City was a blast, as it always is. Vibrant, busy, loud, funny and famous. We climbed the Empire State Building, strolled through Central Park, took a ride on the Staten Island Ferry. We even bumped into Mariah Carey while having breakfast at Trump International Hotel and Tower. To this day I still don't know how she knew we would be there.

Loved Boston and the uber-cool accents. It was my first visit to Beantown, and I remember seeing a squirrel for the very first time in a park near Beacon Hill. Funny little creatures. Even went on a walking ghost tour of the city in the middle of the night that covered the path of the Boston Strangler. And visited a pub where everyone knew my name.

Lenox is a beautiful historic town in the middle of Berkshire County. Lots of boutiques and antiques, and Tanglewood is the summer home of the Boston Symphony Orchestra. We stayed at the impressive Wheatleigh, which is nestled amongst the stunning mountain range. And when the staff nonchalantly remind you to lock the doors facing out because of the bears, they actually mean it.

Stayed overnight in the super cute Manchester Village. I remember picking up some of the best maple syrup I have ever tasted from a cart on the side of the road. A little further down the way, we stopped and had some home-made ice cream from a local farm during the height of summer. Such great, random finds.

I had always wanted to visit Pittsburgh and it did not disappoint. This was my first time in the Steel City and apart from meeting family that we now travel with regularly, the highlight was my wife's uncle pulling some strings to get me on a tour of Heinz Field with locker room access. I was like a kid in a lolly factory.

Philadelphia is known as the City of Brotherly Love and has a great vibe. We did the Rocky Steps, only to wonder who stole the statue when we got to the top. I had enough Philly cheesesteaks to satisfy my curiosity, although I am still not certain whether I prefer Pat's or Geno's. Even caught the subway out to Citizens Bank Park to watch the Phillies play, and realised that this was where they moved the Rocky statue to.

If you are paying attention, then you would have noticed I missed out Niagara Falls. That's because we maybe, possibly, never made it there.

The plan was to stay on the Canadian side, visit the Hershey Chocolate Factory, and sneak in a quick visit to the WWE Store (don't judge me). The next day we had a tour booked to go out on a boat and get all wet under the Falls before heading on our way to Pittsburgh.

The problem was that when we got to the US/Canada border, I was
asked for our passports by a Canada Border Services Agency officer,
or Dudley Do-Right for short. I always keep them in a leather-bound
wallet but I could not find it. No drama, I must have packed them
in a suitcase or bag. So I jumped out of the car, popped open the
boot and started rummaging through our luggage. After about five
minutes, I found the spare tyre, jack, jumper leads, some discarded
chewing gum wrappers, but no passports.

It's about now that I started to get this sinking feeling in the pit of my
stomach that something might be wrong. A little like when you stub
your toe on the dining room table in the middle of the night, wearing
no shoes or socks, during winter.

I naively thought that because we were from Australia, a fellow
Commonwealth country, the Canadian authorities would let us cross
the border while we figured out what happened to our passports.
No such luck, I'm afraid. We were tersely told we could not enter O
Canada O Canada and would have to turn around and go back over
the Rainbow Bridge into the US of A. This is one of the reasons why I
still hold a massive grudge against all Canadians, especially Celine
Dion. Well, to be honest, it wouldn't matter what nationality Celine
Dion was.

Anyway, once we reached the American border, we were met by a
US Border Patrol Agent, or Man Without Sense of Humour, for short.
He explained that they couldn't let us back into the US because we
didn't have our passports.

So there we are. Clowns to the left of me, jokers to the right, literally
stuck in the middle of No Man's Land.

I explained the situation and we were taken to a processing room,
where I did get to the bottom of the missing passport mystery. I
am in charge of the valuables when we travel. By habit, I normally
place everything in the hotel safe once we check in. This includes
passports. It turns out this is exactly what I did at the Wheatleigh in
Lenox, but I had forgotten to open it upon our departure. Thankfully
everything was still locked up in the safe and the hotel organised to
FedEx our belongings straight to Pittsburgh.

Now, depending on who tells this story, it took a few hours for the Border Patrol to get a hold of a Customs Officer who was able to verify our date of arrival into the US. They then electronically sent over a copy of our passport and visas. As we couldn't visit the 51st State of the US, we decided to head to Pittsburgh a day early.

In the other version we were profiled, strip searched, high-pressure hosed down, handcuffed, then ruthlessly interrogated while they were trying to break our resolve so we could tell them the truth about our so-called 'road trip'. They used telephone books, high wattage lamps, good cop/bad cop techniques; but neither of us cracked under pressure so we were placed in a cell with other drug runners, murderers and terrorists. About 5-6 hours later, while everyone was asleep, there was an explosion and the wall beside us caved in. It was Chuck Norris who had come to break us out. We hotwired our car and headed to Pittsburgh a day early. We have been on the run from the authorities ever since, but they will never catch us.

Dear Diary,

In 2002 we travelled to the UK for what was really my first proper visit. Yes, I had transited through Heathrow on a few occasions, even spent a day in London on business, but never really had time to explore and play tourist.

We arrived towards the end of July during the height of summer. I can't remember the exact date but what I do remember distinctly was that the day we landed was declared a heatwave. We were staying at The Franklin in Knightsbridge, a cute little boutique hotel which backs onto Edgerton Gardens. After checking in, I walked past reception and through to the communal garden square, where I literally jumped in fright as I was greeted by a sea of locals lazing on the grass, shirts off, sunbaking in the middle of the day. Welcome to London!

There were two major highlights of that trip. The first was our visit to Manchester.

Because it was the off season, I organised a stadium tour of Old Trafford, home to the greatest football club in the world, Manchester United. The tour was booked for 10am and as it takes approximately 4 hours to drive from London to Manchester, we had to leave around 5.30am just in case we encountered any traffic along the way.

The drive up was without incident and similar to what the English Premier League table should always look like: London clubs in the rear-view mirror, passing all Midlands clubs on your way up, and seeing all teams from the North West near the top. And by teams from the North West, I specifically mean the Red Devils.

It was a typical summer's day in Manchester - cold, overcast and constant drizzle. We arrived ahead of schedule and had time to enjoy a Full English at the Red Café. It was going to be a long day so we needed all the sustenance one could consume.

The tour was everything I expected it to be and The Theatre of Dreams is just that. There is an unmistakable aura that surrounds the stadium that cannot be denied. You sense the nostalgia dripping from the walls as you walk through the corridors. You feel it when visiting the dressing rooms and sitting in the exact same spots that the likes of Robson, Cantona and Scholes had once occupied. And there is magic swirling all around as you head out through the exalted tunnel and onto that hallowed pitch.

Once the tour was finished, we headed into town for a pub lunch and some sightseeing. Manchester also happened to be hosting the Commonwealth Games, and I happened to know a travel writer who happened to give birth to Matt Welsh, who happened to be the Australian world champion swimmer in the backstroke and butterfly. The swimming was being held at the Manchester Aquatics Centre, so we decided to have dinner out on the Curry Mile. We caught a bus from the centre of town and when I asked the ticket inspector how we would know we had reached Wilmslow Road, he just smiled and replied, 'You will know, you will smell it.' We did. And the meal was amazing.

Because of my stellar connections, we sat with the family and friends of all of the Australian swimmers. In fact, we ended up sitting right beside Liesel Jones' mum, who was just delightful. It was amazing seeing the likes of Matt Welsh, Liesel Jones, Grant Hackett and Ian Thorpe live in action and doing Australia proud. Everyone around us must have sensed I was the shy, retiring type because they gave me an Australian flag in hope that it would coax me out of my shell. It worked a treat, as I ended up waving it furiously the entire night and shouting myself hoarse.

The only downside was that the session finished around midnight and we had a 4-hour drive back to London. It also didn't help that we had a tour booked to visit Stonehenge the very next morning and the bus was picking us up at 6am. We had to get to London, drop the hire car off, get to our hotel and squeeze in a couple of hours of sleep before our tour. Reason 793 to use a travel agent.

As we headed down the M6 in the middle of the night, the first couple of hours were fine; the adrenaline was still pumping as we relived the day's events. It was about this time that my eyelids started to feel heavy. I went to ask my co-pilot if she could take over but she was fast asleep. I thought the next best thing would be to wake her and ask her to keep me awake. For the next hour, the conversation went a little like:

'Are you awake?'

'Huh, yes. Um. OK. What?'

'I am feeling sleepy so I need YOU to help ME, and keep me awake.'

Silence...

'Are you awake?'

'Huh, yes. Um. OK. What?'

At this point, I wound the windows all way down to let in the cold, fresh air...I mean, warm summer breeze. I then decided to turn the radio up to MAXIMUM. The most absurd moment came when we're halfway there, as I am driving at 100km/h, I took her hand in mine, I swear, and we stuck our heads out of our respective windows belting out the lyrics to whoa *Living on a Prayer*.

I still don't know how we made it back to London in one piece. All I recollect from the remainder of our journey was taking the wrong exit near Tottenham, getting lost, and then being stopped by a Bobbie at Trafalgar Square. The look of pity on his face when he received a blabbering, exhausted explanation that I was from Australia, lost, trying to find the Avis garage near Knightsbridge so we could make our 6am tour to Stonehenge, brought a tear to my eye. He simply nodded, gave me directions and told me to be careful. Oh, bless his cockney soul.

We eventually found the garage, dropped off the car, headed back to our hotel, and had enough time for a quick shower, a change of clothes and a cup of tea before hopping onto the bus to Stonehenge. I remember nothing of that day apart from being able to walk right up to the monument. There were also some Druids and a sacrifice, but all of that is a little sketchy.

The other highlight of the trip was having breakfast at The Dorchester. If Old Trafford had an aura about it, then The Dorch most certainly does, from those amazing classic and super cars parked out front, to the majestic doormen greeting you, the impressive lobby, and the stunning flower arrangements in the quintessential Promenade. Yet for all its grandeur and legendary status, it had an undeniable warmth and it felt just like home.

And it still does every time I go back.

CHAPTER 6
SEPTEMBER

123-456-789-119

Dear Diary,

Some time later today, when London Town decides to awaken from its slumber, it will mark the first time since March that our entire legendary gang of hotels are back open and together.

Ergo, I am in a celebratory mood - yet there will be no adult beverages for me tonight. Well, maybe just one or two. I do enjoy the odd tipple here and there, but I do have to remind myself not to over-indulge, for several reasons. Liquid satisfaction is temporary after all, yet its effects can be everlasting. Let me explain.

We have been a long-time supporter of the Olivia Newton-John Foundation, and back in 2015 I got all dolled up in black to attend the ONJ Gala in Melbourne.

For those wondering, yes, I have rubbed shoulders with the lady that many a teenage boy was Hopelessly Devoted to after watching her strut her stuff in *Grease* as Sandy. My claim to fame, in fact, is sharing a toastie with Olivia; although I am happy to report (especially as we are now living in a Covid-19 world) that I had no chills and they were never multiplying.

The evening was a huge success, but for whatever reason, I somehow ended up drinking a little more than I normally would. You see, I am a sucker for a good silent auction and have ended up bidding and winning several items down the years, including concert tickets, Chef's Tables, artwork and (more) wine.

This particular evening, there was on offer a VIP Experience to the upcoming Neil Diamond concert.

I Am, I Said, a fan but not what you would call a devotee. My wife is, though, and as the date of his concert was in the same month as her birthday, I decided to surprise her with the two tickets offered for auction.

Like a lion stalking his prey, I was the ultimate apex predator, methodically circling his quest. To the untrained eye, I was just another charitable soul in a dinner suit who just happened to be randomly walking past the auction table with a glass of red wine in his hand. Yet to a seasoned gala auction bidder, I had walked by maybe fourteen times too many for this to be an arbitrary coincidence.

It is no surprise, then, that I ended up being the winning bidder, so I exited the evening in a limousine, with Olivia and her entourage in tow and a prize-winning envelope in hand.

What was a surprise was when I opened up the envelope the very next morning and discovered that the concert I had bid for and won the night before, was in fact for his Melbourne show.

In hindsight, that should not have been such a revelation, seeing that I was in Melbourne; but the adrenaline and perhaps the Red, Red Wine had dulled my powers of deduction.

A quick check of my calendar revealed that the concert was on a Thursday night. Very doable. Unfortunately, that same week I was due to be in Brisbane for work. We have a problem, Houston. I was determined not to let this little detail defeat my best intentions, and although I may not bring her flowers anymore, I was going to bring my wife to a Neil Diamond concert.

So we talked it over and I hatched an ingenious plan. Early Monday morning on the week of the concert, I flew up to Brisbane for my sales mission and hit the ground running. On Thursday morning, my wife flew down to Melbourne for some retail therapy before checking in to The Lyall. That same morning, I checked out of my hotel in Brisbane, attended to my meetings during the day, and then drove to the airport in the afternoon so I could fly down to Melbourne and join her. Once my plane landed, I jumped into a taxi and headed to the hotel. I made it with just enough time for a quick shower and change of clothes, and was back in a taxi, heading to Rod Laver Arena for our VIP Experience.

The tickets included dinner prior to the concert, a souvenir pack and two seats just a few rows from the front of the stage. For a 74yo (at the time), Neil Diamond put on a hell of a show. It was much more than just a Beautiful Noise, as he performed for almost two hours, sang all of his hits and had everyone - and I do mean everyone, young and old - up off their seats, dancing and singing along for the entire night. I surprised myself with how many songs I actually knew and it still ranks as one of my Top 5 concerts of all time.

When he finally walked off stage sometime around 11pm, we headed back to our hotel. The next morning my wife slept in, had a leisurely breakfast, and was able to fly back to Sydney at a decent time.

In contrast, I was up at 5am just so I could jump into a taxi, head to the airport and fly back up to Brisbane as I still had some meetings to attend on Friday morning. When I eventually finished my calls, I drove back to the airport to catch my original flight back home to Sydney.

Exhausting yet unforgettable. And I am thankful for two legends, Olivia and Neil, who helped create such a memorable adventure.

And I can't wait to say Hello Again to all our legendary hotels.

Dear Diary,

Earlier this week, Manchester United launched their new season third kit. There is a lot of money to be made in merchandising because these days every football team has a home strip, an away strip, and a third strip just in case you haven't spent enough already.

Some say the design makes the players look like zebras roaming around in the wild, while others say it makes them look like convicts in a prison yard. I tend to side with the latter view, and not just because some of their players misbehaved during the off season and have had run-ins with the law.

I believe whoever designed the strip at Adidas is making a political statement that we all feel like prisoners during this pandemic. Either that or they have been smoking something with amazing hallucinogenic properties.

And contrary to many rumours, I have only seen the inside of a prison cell three times in my entire life and each occasion has left an indelible mark on me.

The most recent time was in 2017 when I visited the former penal colony of Port Arthur, which is about a 90-minute drive southeast from Hobart, Tasmania. It has a rich history on its own because from around 1830 it was home to Britain's most dangerous convicts (who were sent to Australia), and it is now a World Heritage listed Historic Site. But it will forever be linked to the mass shooting that occurred there in 1996. It is beautiful, eerie, silent and harrowing all at once. I found it to be such a forlorn site, and the lost souls there are yet to find peace.

The second time was in 2008 when I visited Robben Island, which is roughly an hour by ferry north of Cape Town. As you depart and look back, what farewells you is the dramatic and stunning view of

Table Mountain towering over the V&A Waterfront. In stark contrast, Robben Island is both barren and bleak; yet it is one of the most spiritual places I have ever visited. I can only describe Mandela's 8ft by 7ft cell as a true place of worship, for only a divine right would have filled this man with the strength and courage to endure for so long.

And the first time was in 2007, when I visited Alcatraz Island located in the San Francisco Bay.

I had seen both the *Birdman of Alcatraz* with Burt Lancaster and of course *Escape from Alcatraz* starring Clint Eastwood, so I knew some of the history of the prison and its claim to be escape-proof. It also housed some of America's most notorious criminals such as Robert Stroud (the real 'Birdman'), Al Capone and George 'Machine Gun' Kelly. You are overcome by such a sombre feeling the moment you land on the island and it prompted me to write the following:

New Year's Eve

As the wind swept across the bay
They could hear the laughter
And the music
Of their freedom.

It rolled in slowly
Through the cracked vents
And trickled down
Along the damp walls.

Fragile hands wrapped feebly
Around solid bars,
Drawn faces pressed harshly
Against cool metal,
Blistered lips
Counting down in unison
To midnight.
Hollow eyes shut tight,
Praying in silence
That they too
Were ushering in
A new beginning.

Just like those
Imprisoned souls
On Alcatraz
Who withered away
In solitude,
My heart
Calls out for you.
I am so close
Allow me please
To reach out
And touch you,
Make you believe
That what I taste
Is in reality
Our freedom.

I know that at times it feels like you are trapped and imprisoned, but this is not reality. We all have our families, our friends and our colleagues to help us through these tough times. And we WILL get through this.

And things could be much worse. Just search up the new Manchester United third kit and imagine being made to wear that out in public.

Dear Diary,

In 2014, I fulfilled a life-long dream of becoming a tag-along spouse and I couldn't have been happier.

See, my wife needed to attend a medical conference in Cancun, Mexico, and we decided to plan our family holiday around this.

I am not certain why it appealed to me so much, but I had forever dreamt of sleeping in while my better half rose early to attend her meetings, allowing me to strut in late to breakfast wearing flip flops, a Hawaiian shirt and a Borsalino. The fantasy would be completed by dropping off my daughter to the Kid's Club and then lazing around the pool all day, swimming up to the bar every once in a while and ordering fancy cocktails with colourful little umbrellas in them.

We stayed at the recently opened NIZUC Resort and Spa on the Punta Nizuc, which is conveniently located just out of town. Apart from visiting Tulum, Chichen Itza, and swimming in as many cenotes as possible, on top of my Cancun To Do list was snorkelling at MUSA: the Underwater Museum of Art. MUSA was the brain child of conservationists who were slowly seeing the coral reefs in Cancun damaged by tourists, anchors, snorkellers and divers. It was and continues to be an ingenious way of regenerating the coral in the area. By submerging more than 500 sculptures by Mexican and international artists, the coral attaches to the art and over time grows to form a new reef. It is living art in conservation, and promotes both nature and art simultaneously

Unfortunately, the day we visited, MUSA was extremely windy and the boat ride out to the site was an adventure on its own. The sea was angry and our guides seriously contemplated calling our visit off. They decided we could proceed but we were all made to wear life vests.

Once in the water, you could swim with fervour and not move an inch. Yet if stationary, within seconds you would easily find yourself 10-15 metres away from where you had begun. It made snorkelling extremely difficult but with some determination and perseverance, the beauty of the sculptures became evident, from the stunning *Reclamation* with her hands triumphantly held up high towards the surface, to the strangely calming *Athropocene* where a child sleeps peacefully on the windshield of VW Beetle, to the striking *The Anchors* when your heart skips a beat as you discover that one face staring ominously up at you.

On this fateful day just prior to the start of the conference, one of the doctors decided to join us. The doctor in question is a wife, a mother, and an expert in her field of medicine. I was caught off guard when I turned around and saw her panicking in the water, floating further and further away from our boat. Her hands were waving frantically above her head, and despite the life vest she was wearing, she was starting to go under. I swam over to her as fast as I could, grabbed her vest and dragged her back towards the boat, where one of the guides helped me get her back on board.

When she had calmed down, I asked her what had happened and she matter-of-factly explained that she couldn't swim. That was the very first time she had mentioned this insignificant little detail, so I asked her why she had come along in the first place. Her answer? She didn't want to miss out.

Call it FOMO or call it tourists forgetting their inhibitions in a foreign land, but I was perplexed. When we flew back to Australia, her husband thanked me for saving her life and then also told me how she never even enters the pool with their children, let alone try and swim in the ocean. He even jokingly (I think) said that I should have just left her there if she was silly enough to get in the water in the first place.

There was also another instance in Cancun when we were out for lunch. My wife got a call from another doctor in a panic; he had apparently had a 'small' accident on a jet ski and needed the details to their international medical insurance from his wife, who happened to be with us but whose phone was switched off.

He also had never (ever) been on a jet ski but had decided to go out with another tag-along spouse (do you see a pattern forming here?) who obviously knew what he was doing.

We caught a cab over to the scene of the crime, and when we arrived the doctor was arguing with the owner of the jet ski hire company, while the jet ski was perched upside down about 200 metres behind him, on some jagged rocks beyond the water. Apparently, when the owner of the jet ski hire company said to the doctor, 'See those rocks over there, don't go anywhere near them,' the doctor decided he needed to take a closer look at where he wasn't supposed to go. He left Mexico bruised, battered and about $10K lighter.

Why am I telling you all this? Well, the one thing that I have learnt in 2020 is that problem solving needs to be attacked on several fronts. To form strategies, we need the expertise of many. By this I mean that we should not just rely on one individual or sector to make all-encompassing decisions that affect an entire society. We should be listening to health care professionals, economists, business leaders, and even our politicians, to come up with solutions.

There is balance needed that can only be met by consulting many.

Dear Diary,

I went to pick up my dry cleaning yesterday and noticed that the festive season had well and truly arrived at my local shopping centre.

There are still about 100 days to go but the signs are up, sharing the details of when it is deemed acceptable (in any other year) to line up with other responsible adults, just to place your child on the knee of a stranger who happens to be in disguise, and then pay them a king's ransom for the evidence.

That also means the decorations won't be far behind, and the supermarkets have already stocked their shelves with cards, wrapping paper, puddings, mince pies and iced fruit cakes.

Yet no matter whether you celebrate Hanukkah, Christmas, Geeta Jayanti or the Winter/Summer Solstice, I am not sure that we are going to be in much of a celebratory mood come December this year.

In fact, I believe that the holiday season is going to feel a little like the ending of the original 1968 *Planet of the Apes* movie. The one where Charlton Heston stumbles across the remains of the Statue of Liberty and realises that the 'alien' planet ruled by Apes that he thought he was stranded on, was in fact his very own post-apocalyptic Earth: 'Damn them, damn them all to hell!'

There will be no naughty or nice lists this year as these have been replaced by open or closed border lists. Frankincense, myrrh and gold have been replaced by face masks, hand sanitiser and alcohol. Speaking of which, eggnog will make a BIG comeback, with a lot more nog than egg. And with our COVID kilos piling on, many of us will be over-qualified to play Santa this year; but to be fair, I think we would much rather be breaking out of our homes than breaking back into one.

The one thing I can definitely do without are all the dreadful Christmas songs. I know the English have an infatuation with them, but I have never really been one for festive tunes. I'm not 100% certain why; but it may have something to do with being stuck in traffic for over an hour one year, in the back seat of my boss's 3-door Celica Coupe, on our way to our end-of-year lunch, listening to Mariah Carey's Christmas album on loop. Enough to drive anyone insane.

Of the few that I do enjoy, my favourite has to be Paul Kelly's *How to Make Gravy*. That would closely be followed by The Pogues' *Fairytale of New York* and The Ramones' *Merry Christmas (I Don't Want to Fight Tonight)*. But the one song that always makes me smile and that I think really sums up 2020, has to be *The Season Is Upon Us* by the Dropkick Murphys.

And what do you even get someone who has been in lockdown, anyway? Maybe a world globe instead of a snow globe? Forget cryptocurrency. Try transferring Frequent Flyer points to loved ones this year as it is now seen as a long-term investment strategy. And I am certain there will be a lot of re-gifting going on with the number of useless items we have all bought online out of boredom. Yet the ultimate gift would have to be if we were able to replace all the Christmas lights with airport runway lights. As Kevin Costner once said, 'If you build it, they will come.'

If I could choose anywhere in the world to spend the holidays, it would be with my family at Coworth Park in Ascot. It just looks so magical at this time of year and it is your very own Winter Wonderland. For whatever reason, it reminds me of the movie classic *Holiday Inn* starring Bing Crosby and Fred Astaire.

And yes, I know we can't get there this year, but I am still adding it to my travel bucket list for future reference.

CHAPTER 7
OCTOBER

Dear Diary,

Recently I confessed to you that I had the pleasure of sharing a limousine and a toastie with Sandy from *Grease*. Well in the scheme of things, there are worse things I could do (apologies, I couldn't help myself).

That got me thinking about some of the 'famous' people I have met down the years on my travels. This is by no means a definitive list, but just some examples that came to mind while reminiscing.

In 2007, John Travolta and Kelly Preston met me at The Kahala in Hawaii. My daughter was taking a nap and I had stepped out of our room and into the corridor to answer a call. As I was yapping away, sounding all important, a couple walked past me holding hands, and I noticed that the gentleman was smiling at me intently. We both nodded and acknowledged each other and it took me a few seconds to realise that the gentleman was indeed Danny Zuko in the flesh. I have always assumed he was smiling because he recognised my accent and not because he thought I was just a self-absorbed douche bag on a phone. Thinking laterally, he would be particularly familiar with the Australian accent, not only owing to his old Rydell High flame. John Travolta has been a Qantas Ambassador for many years and owns and pilots his own QF Boeing 707. There is even footage of him celebrating in the dressing rooms with the triumphant Qantas Socceroos when they defeated Uruguay back in 2005, to qualify for the World Cup after a 32-year absence.

Also in Hawaii and also at The Kahala but this time in 2009, we had the pleasure of spending some quality time with our good friends Rihanna, Jay-Z and Kanye West. They were on the island recording Rihanna's latest album and we were there holidaying with family, but we made it a point to connect every morning at breakfast. To this day, my wife's cousin still tells everyone that he shared a meal with Rihanna. Well, technically he did, because on the first day she did walk right up to him and asked if where he was standing was the egg station. She then proceeded to stand beside him while they waited for their respective omelettes to be cooked. The two things that I remember vividly were the size of her bodyguard (one of the largest human beings I have ever laid eyes on) and the amount of food he consumed on a daily basis, sitting at a table all by himself. He was incredibly polite too, and far from a Rude Boy (there I go again).

For all the Australian soap opera fans, I met Leah Patterson (Ada Nicodemou) from *Home and Away* in Italy. It was 2001 and she and a friend were staying at the same hotel as ours in Milan. I took the liberty of introducing myself as I could see they recognised me and were contemplating whether they should approach. We got acquainted over drinks and all went out to dinner together. We even caught up again in Venice a few days later and did the whole thing again.

As I have previously shared with you, Mariah Carey was stalking us in New York City in 2004. What I neglected to tell you was that on the very same trip we also met Venus Williams in the lobby of The Peninsula, and Vin Diesel (literally) on Broadway. It's so difficult to remain under the radar at times.

Back in 2013, I met Mrs Koothrappali (Alice Amter) from *The Big Bang Theory* at The Original Farmers Market in LA. I love the vibe of that place and had made my way to one of the outside bars; it was Sunday after all, I had just landed earlier in the day, it was St Patrick's Day, and the LA Marathon had just been run. I had no idea who she was at the time as I didn't really watch the show, but we got on famously. She was so lovely and was nice enough to give me a lift back to The Beverly Hills Hotel where I was staying. I offered to buy her a drink in The Polo Lounge to say thank you for the lift and just as we sat down, in walked Chris Rock who had apparently been looking for me all day. He does have my number, so not sure what game he was playing at.

I have been fortunate enough to meet many famous, important and influential people at all of our hotels, but the Pink Palace still has to be the one where I have had the most sightings. Down the years I have met the likes of Yoko Ono, Jennifer Garner, Diane Keaton, and Victoria Beckham, who quite literally bumped into me at The Polo Lounge. I always had a thing for Posh Spice, although it might have had more to do with the fact that she is married to David 'Golden Balls' Beckham and my love for Manchester United. Suffice to say she apologised and then proceeded to tell me what she wanted, what she really, really wanted for lunch (I promise, that was the last one).

I also remember hosting a lunch there with clients while Mark Wahlberg happened to be on the table beside us pitching his next movie concept to a table full of financiers. I made the mistake of telling the group to remain calm and inconspicuous. And over the next hour there were at least 43 trips to the bathroom. I learnt my lesson well.

Not sure about you, but I have always wondered whether famous people get nervous when they meet other famous people? If you get the chance, there is a wonderful interview with Michael Caine on *The Graham Norton Show* where he tells the hilarious story of when he met John Wayne at The Beverly Hills Hotel. Priceless.

Dear Diary,

I have nothing this week. No amusing tales from my past travels. No witty idioms or strange anecdotes to regale you with.

If I am honest, I have felt a little drained, forlorn and defeated, just because. My confidence in our so-called leaders is at an all-time low as it becomes increasingly apparent they are only interested in saving their own skin. Yet I have to remind myself that the bar was set quite low to begin with

It's just been a trying week for no reason in particular. And that is OK. Dare I say, it might even be normal.

My one solace has been getting out and seeing as many clients as I can in person. Or jumping on the phone and having a chat about everything and nothing. What buoys me is their determination and resolve and love for what we do.

So I am glad the weekend is almost here.

PS. OK, you twisted my arm. Here is something I just wrote:

Dr Who?

They have a plan.
It is quite grand,
A plan that strands
A travel ban.

Their plan I swear
Tied our hands.
No sand,
No tan
No foreign lands!

I wish to ban
Their plan that can
Stop sand and tans
And trips to Cannes.

Shall I use a van
To ram their plan,
Perhaps a hitman
Named Leanne?

I will
Brand them
With a pan,
I will
Slam them
Like Van Damme,
I will
Stand on
All their glands.

So I can
Stick it
To the man
And ban their
Master Plan!

Dear Diary,

In just over a week, Year 12 students in high schools all around Australia will sit for their final round of exams. There has always been enormous pressure associated with these exams, as they form the major portion of the mark which dictates whether students are accepted into university to pursue their chosen field.

This year I can't even begin to imagine the stress, chaos, confusion and upheaval these students have had to deal with in addition to the 'normal' academic pressures. Meanwhile, our politicians are mortgaging their futures by increasing fees for certain degrees simply to pander to schools that have become businesses, which care more about profit and loss statements and the money they receive from their foreign student intake than about being the institutions they were meant to be - places of higher education for all.

I know some may scoff at my idealism, but in Australia from 1974-1989, there were no university fees attached to tertiary education. Some of you may be even more surprised to learn that I was not one of those privileged students who was able to study for free. How old do you really think I am?

I spent the bulk of my three years studying Communications at the University at Western Sydney (UWS), Werrington campus. It was a 40-minute drive from my home, but in the beginning I used to catch the train which took about 90-minutes door to door. I would catch the bus near our house, head to Eastwood station, board one train, then change to another at Strathfield so I could continue on my merry way to Werrington. I remember one of the first times I made the trip, I was sitting quietly minding my own business, when I heard music emanating from somewhere near the rear of the convoy. Up I got to investigate, and walked through multiple carriages following the sound, until I found a bunch of misfits singing acapella to some old Motown songs. I always sat in that carriage from that day forward.

Once at Werrington Station, we would walk off the platform and hike uphill in single file for 10 minutes to get to our campus. It felt like we were sheep being herded from one paddock to another. No questions asked. I know that you are probably thinking this is a little ritualistic for free-spirited university students. And I would tend to agree. But I neglected to tell you that my old campus is located next to Cobham Youth Justice Centre, which is basically a remand centre for males aged 15yo and over. I think we would rather have been sheep than head to the wrong institution. Although I do often wonder what kind of debt I would have accrued had I taken the other path...

Even though our campus was quite small, you were greeted by a long, straight road as you entered off the main highway. You could say it was somewhat similar to what you might expect to see in a British period film, as the heroine is driven down the imposing grand path for the very first time to the old English manor which shall be her home for the next three years. Actually, come to think of it, it does remind me a little of Coworth Park in Ascot. Just replace the Kids' Club with the Dean's House as you enter. Replace the polo fields with a large, nondescript student car park. The mansion would be our main D Block Building, where Admin and the Lecture Hall were. And the jewel in the crown, The Dower House, would be our Cafeteria. We even had a lake, although ours was man-made.

Sometime during Year 2, I started ditching the train and driving more. That led to quicker journeys, and joy rides around the student carpark with as many people as we could fit in the boot of my father's 1978 Ford Fairlane. I think the record was 6 people snugly contorted in the boot. Door shut. They certainly don't make cars like they used to.

Despite the fact that it was after sitting in my very first lecture that I realised I couldn't read a thing and needed glasses, I do have very fond memories of my days at UWS.

From the heated discussions about religion, equality, capitalism and socialism in the cafeteria, to the demonstrations and protests on and off campus.

From the live music and crazy harbour cruises to playing pool at Werrington Pub with the locals, wearing my 'they looked like a good idea at the time' MC Hammer pants.

From pulling an all-nighter just to finish off an assignment on my sister's electric typewriter and then driving 40 minutes just to hand it in, to joining the University basketball team and voluntarily doing that same drive several times a week.

From following a Sydney hard rock band around for a month, as we filmed a documentary which they included in a video/CD pack, to working as an intern one day a week at Markson Sparks! and working for several well-known personalities.

It is also where I got my love for writing. Apart from the assignments and essays, we would write scripts and 'How To' manuals and learn to edit. I even ended up writing a regular column for the campus newspaper. Although my *pièce de résistance* had to be rewriting the lyrics to *Bohemian Rhapsody* and performing it in front of the year while my lecturer slowly backed away in fear as I climbed onto chairs and tables singing my epic ode to her (just replace *Mama* with *Marcia* and you sort of get the idea).

Yet the irony of all ironies is that I was on the organising committee for our graduation party, which was held at the old Swiss Grand Hotel in Bondi. I guess my cards were marked from the start as to which industry I would end up in.

So spare a thought for anyone sitting for their university entrance exams this year. And remember, no matter what your situation, never ever stop learning.

> *Live as if you were to die tomorrow. Learn as it you were to live forever.*
>
> - Mahatma Gandhi

Dear Diary,

As I am unable to travel physically at this present moment in time, I decided to journey extensively to my Frontal, Parietal, Occipital and Temporal Lobes instead.

Or, in other words, just some scattered thoughts from my troubled mind this week:

In the socially distanced world that we now live in, I wonder what the politically correct term for a *Flash Mob* is? Would *Covered Individuals* be more appropriate? Not very appealing or exciting, but I imagine that coordinating one now would be a walk in the park.

I am all for recycling, so I believe suffering from ADHD should now also mean one can endure an acute case of *Anticlimactic Domicile Homestay Disease*.

I would like to take a moment and raise a glass to salute all the fallen fondue and shabu-shabu restaurants of the world. Alas, poor eateries, I knew thee well and thy delectable morsels shalt be missed. Farewell, fair cruelty, for parting is such sweet sorrow.

Once upon a time, in a land before the internets, conspiracy theorists theorised that Diana Ross and Michael Jackson were in fact one and the same and interchangeable. Yet I ask the question, has anyone ever seen Boris Johnson, Donald Trump and Gary Busey all in the same room, at the same time? I do believe that this creepy trio of doppelgangers have world domination in their sights, and their scheming surely explains all the incoherent press conferences and late-night Twitter tirades.

While I am on a somewhat similar tangent, what is it with world leaders and their crazy hairstyles? I am not one to normally comment on such matters because 1) people think I am just exhibiting a cranial jealous streak, and 2) they say I am spreading heresy. But if you glance over to the UK, to the USA, to North Korea, to Germany - do these people not own mirrors in their homes? And to think they have 'people' who are paid to look after their appearance. Just more wasted taxpayer dollars.

One activity that I have taken up again in 2020 is heading back to the future and playing squash. And before you ask, yes, people do still play squash. I swear, if I had a dollar for every time someone asked me that, I would have enough money to buy new batteries for my Walkman. I am thoroughly enjoying myself but I am not so sure about my opponents. I had one friend whose knee blew up like a balloon and I have not seen him since. Then I have another who over the last two months has pulled a calf muscle, strained a muscle in his forearm, and just last week ended up in Emergency at Westmead Hospital after a ball hit him flush in his eye and caused a haematoma. Thankfully I was not the one who inflicted the damage, but his wife and I are not on speaking terms at present. I thought I was doing the right thing by checking in on his wellbeing, although I may have crossed the line when I asked if he would be OK to play again next week.

It is 30 years since I finished high school. In fact, on August 15th we were supposed to have our 30-Year Reunion but a little pandemic got in the way. As a result, only five of us braved the conditions for a quiet drink at our old local watering hole. Our 30-Year Reunion (Part II) has been rescheduled for next month, although I fear that those who now live interstate will still not be able to attend. And a 31-Year Reunion just doesn't have the same appeal to it.

Having reconnected with a few old school friends, I got to thinking about those days of old, and in particular my mindset at the time. I knew pretty early on that I wanted to study Communications at university, which I reminisced about last week. At the time, it was more the radio/TV/broadcasting aspect that I was enamoured with. Little wonder, then, that I loved performing and took Drama as an elective. I really enjoyed the production side of things, but I still ended up playing Vince Fontaine in our school production of *Grease* (three nights only, completely sold out, standing room only, the local scalpers made a killing) and Tom in Michael Gow's *Away*. You could say that I was always destined to get into drama and theatre, so the travel industry was just a logical progression.

Speaking of thespian pursuits, around this time last year I hosted a trip to Paris and London with British Airways. Our first stop was Paris, and while we were checking in to the Hotel Plaza Athénée, we were literally met at reception by video cameras, boom mics and light reflectors. Those who know appreciate that we greet ALL our guests like movie stars and that I did not tip off the local paparazzi about our impending arrival. Yet in the end, I did have to confess that they may or may not have just witnessed a new Netflix series being filmed about a certain *Emily in Paris*.

And I can (sort of) let you in on another little secret, especially if you find yourself in the Eternal City next February. If are in Rome at that time, then you might like to head on over to Hotel Eden to catch a glimpse of Patrick Dempsey filming Season 2 of his financial thriller *Devils*.

Dear Diary,

Some two thousand years ago, just before I was born, Celtic pagans celebrated the end of the harvest and summer season with a three-day festival. It was a time of celebration and thanks, but also one which ushered in the telling winter solstice. This festival was called Samhain.

Samhain was a fire festival which commenced on October 31st, and the Celts would light bonfires to mark the beginning of the dark half of the year. Villagers would attend these celebrations wearing costumes made of animal heads and skin. It was also believed that spirits and ghosts returned to the earth at this time, so food was left outside their doors as offerings to appease uninvited souls.

In 49 AD the Romans, who had now conquered most of the Celtic lands, introduced their own festival called Feralia, which honoured the passing of the dead. This was also observed during the month of October.

Then in 609 AD, the Catholic Church introduced All Saints Day on May 13th. A few hundred years later, they consciously moved this celebration to November 1st, praying it would replace the old popular pagan festival of Samhain. This makes perfect sense once you are aware that paganism was never really a religion but rather a derogatory term used by Christianity to label any 'ungodly' practices that were the antithesis of their own beliefs. It then morphed into a type of dogma describing anyone who practised an unfamiliar religion or polytheism.

At the time, All Saints Day was also referred to as All Hallows Day, and thus the night before became known as All Hallows Eve. Fast forward to today, add in a tincture of commercialism (I said a touch… oops too much) and hello Daddy, Halloween as we know it was born.

Halloween can be viewed as a melding of both Samhain and All Saints Day, for it is difficult to know where old customs cease and where modern tradition begins. You can see this clearly in Mexico and the imagery the locals use to celebrate the Day of the Dead (Dia de los Muertos).

Yet the greatest paradox is that we have now come full circle. Modern paganism, the way I understand it, is incredibly holistic and has its roots embedded in nature and the five elements: spirit, air, earth, fire and water. This is not dissimilar to the harmony that we as a world are searching to achieve. However, Halloween is now associated with consumerism, demons, darkness, evil and excess.

Now that your Halloween history lesson is complete (there will be questions at the end), and seeing that today is October 30th, it got me thinking about my own All Hallows Eve experiences. If I am honest, there are only a few.

One reason is that we don't really celebrate Halloween in Australia. It has only started to become a 'thing' over the last 10 years or so. Another is that I live in a street that has very few families. Allow me to rephrase that; I live in a street that has very few families with small children. There are mainly empty nesters or kids that are 18+. As a result, the one and only year my daughter and I tried going door to door to trick or treat, we were met with some very confused and annoyed looks.

So in 2015, when we were invited by our friends to their annual Halloween Street Party, we accepted gleefully. Let me be clear, this gathering is mainly for the kids in the street and provides them with a safe environment to get dressed up and go from house to house asking semi-strangers for candy. Yet it's the adults that seem to have the most fun mingling in their driveways, drinking on a school night, handing out lollies and a few well-meaning insults to the neighbours' children about their costumes. This environment also encourages grownups to dress up, so I decided to put my recently purchased luchador mask (bought in Cancun the year prior) to good use. I accessorised and layered with intent: brightly coloured swimming trunks over black compression tights, lace-up leather boots, a compression top, my lucha libre mask, and *voilà* – El Transit Jr was born. I was banned from administering any suplexes or body slams, but I did get in a few *tope suicidas* over the fence, and at least one tornado DDT. I showed those fledglings *cero miedo*!

My favourite experience, though, was back in 2011 when I hosted a trip with United Airlines to New York City and Los Angeles. First stop was New York City as these were the days when we still owned the New York Palace. After almost getting snowed in at JFK Airport (ours was the last plane to depart before the rest of the days' flights were cancelled), we arrived in sunny Los Angeles and stayed at both the Hotel Bel-Air and The Beverly Hills Hotel.

I know most Hollywood movies focus on the immense Christmas decorations, but Halloween decorations are a sight to behold. It was amazing to see to what extent so many of the locals had gone, to decorate their homes. No expense was spared.

October 31st happened to be while we were at The Beverly Hills Hotel and after a brief discussion, the entire group decided to join in on the festivities. We stopped off at one of the many pop-up costume stores in West Hollywood to pick up appropriate ensembles and by the time we were finished, our gang consisted of a witch, a demon, a pumpkin, a pirate, and me all decked out with my cape, Guy Fawkes mask and *V for Vendetta* hat.

We were now ready for our red-carpet photoshoot outside the Pink Palace. Once this was complete, we descended on the WEHO Halloween Carnival, which is a huge street party full of live music, food, dancing, laughs and some of the best and silliest costumes you would ever hope to see. The remainder of that night is a little hazy, although I do believe I helped overthrow a tyrannical and fascist government.

CHAPTER 8
NOVEMBER

Dear Diary,

This week I spent most of my time coming up with radical ideas on how to stimulate tourism once all the international borders have reopened.

Over the last couple of months, I have read countless research articles highlighting that the tourism sector will rebound easily. It is a given that we will see an increase in domestic travel, and this has already started in earnest. But I was also extremely encouraged to read that these studies show that the sentiment for international travel is as high as 80%.

So my task was clear and precise. How do we attract these international travellers?

My first thought was the wedding market. Surely after being in lockdown and being forced to live in close contact with the same person, seeing them day in, day out for months on end, unwed couples would be champing at the bit to tie the knot. After all, the first mass tourism trend (between 1880-1914) was in fact the honeymoon.

The term *honeymoon* is quite an intriguing one and derives from ancient Babylon, where for the first month after the wedding, the bride's father would give the groom as much mead (honey beer) as he wanted. This became to be known as the Honey Month, and evolved into the Honey Moon because of their lunar calendar.

By the early 19th Century, the British would take a sort of bridal tour and go around visiting friends and family who had been unable to attend their actual wedding. It finally developed into the concept we know today from the French, where couples would depart during their reception to catch a train or ship for their sojourn.

In 1999, I too got married, and we headed to Greece for our honeymoon: Athens, Crete, Paros, Santorini.

In Athens, I followed the British definition above and visited family who were unable to attend our wedding. Athens is always a blast, but nothing out of the ordinary ensued; just lots of sightseeing, laughs, ouzo, dancing and smashing of plates. But then things got really interesting.

First stop was Crete, which is the largest of the Greek isles and is known for its diverse flora and fauna. It is rich in history, mythology, archaeological sites and its stunning natural landscape. We were staying in the capital of Heraklion and I had hired a car so we could explore the secrets of this vast island. On this particular day, we were on our way to a local beach when the fauna decided to get up close and personal. I was wearing shorts and a short sleeve shirt, and my new bride was wearing a tennis dress with her swimming costume underneath. As I was driving along, windows rolled down, inhaling the summer sun and relishing our surroundings, my wife suddenly screamed out in pain. I screeched to a halt and moved over to the side of the road to see what had just transpired. Apparently one of the local bees had taken a liking to her sweet scent and got sucked into the vortex caused by my Fiat Punto as I sped by. It got wedged between her and the seat, got scared and stung her through her dress, between her shoulder blades. I know this because as she got out of the car, the bee fell onto her seat. Dead.

I will pause here to let you know that this was the exact same time my wife decided to reveal to me that despite her love of honey, she was actually allergic to bees. Still in pain and now a little frantic, she told me I would need to take the stinger out. I could see part of it stuck in the fabric of her dress; but to make certain that none of its barbed lancets were still lodged in her back, she lifted her dress up over her head as all the while cars continued to drive by, honking their horns and yelling words of encouragement that thankfully only I could understand. I was able to get most of it out, but we decided to stop off at a chemist in the nearest township just to make sure and to grab some antihistamines. I had to translate the entire scenario to the pharmacist and while he made sure that all of the stinger was removed, I was left beating away the local octogenarians who were gravitating to the back of the store also wanting to lend a hand.

Next stop was Paros, which has always been one of my favourite islands to visit. From the vibrant capital of Parikia, to the lively port of Naoussa, I just love the energy of this paradise. It is home to some fabulous beaches, stunning coastlines and the incredibly hypnotic Valley of the Butterflies. We were staying at Naoussa, so had made our way into Parikia to catch a ferry across to Antiparos. Antiparos is a (very) small island just one nautical mile from Paros with a completely laid-back vibe. We got to the port a little early and were sitting in a local café sipping on a frappé and having some breakfast. Sitting opposite us was a family of sorts - a lady, two older men and a small girl. One of the men suddenly started convulsing, and fell off his chair and onto the ground. We later discovered he was has having an epileptic fit but at the time, confusion and panic set in as none of his clan knew what to do. My wife called out some instructions to keep him calm and ensure that he didn't hurt himself and didn't swallow his tongue. As I translated, his friend decided that this equated to slapping him across his face a couple of times to keep him calm (while yelling his name), hitting him hard on his back with his hand to make sure he didn't hurt himself, and then grabbing a bunch of keys and cramming them in his mouth to make sure he didn't swallow his tongue. It was while this poor man had several keys stuffed in his mouth that my wife decided to step in. As his seizure subsided, she calmly turned him over on his side, got him some water and told his family (through me) to get him up but only when he was feeling ready and OK. We still made it on board to our ferry (just) and across to Antiparos.

Our last destination was Santorini, which is known as the most idyllic of all the Greek Islands. Painted by a volcano, everything about this island is stunning, from the blue and white houses perched perfectly along the cliffside to the black and red sand-laced beaches. We stayed just outside the capital of Fira, but I had organised for us to have dinner one night in Oia. Oia is known for its breathtakingly beautiful sunsets where you can seemingly reach out and touch that

big, red luminous orb, or so it seems. Dinner was at a local *taverna* located at the bottom at Amoudi Bay, where the local fishing boats come in with the day's catch and you get to choose, then and there, what you are going to eat.

There are 200 steps from the top to the bottom and we decided to walk down. One thing that I learnt very quickly was that my new bride had a penchant for glass sculptures, and at the top there was a store which sold some very unique glassware, so we stopped to have a look. All the pieces were by local artists and there was one in particular that caught her eye. I spoke to the owner and pointed to the one we would like to buy - a glass sculpture of a man and woman interwoven as one. The owner picked it up and as we made our way to the front of the store, he suddenly tripped and began to lose his balance. Now, you must remember, in this store everything was made of glass, including the counter at the front. As he stumbled, the sculpture slipped out of his hands and everything changed to slow motion – a little like the *Matrix* minus the sleek black leather coats. I remember reaching out trying to grab the sculpture while seeing it slowly descend and come crashing down onto the glass counter top. The sculpture broke and so did the counter, and shards of glass flew everywhere.

The man was now extremely embarrassed and as he turned around, he saw blood flowing freely from my hand, as some of the shards had sliced open my palm. He was now distraught that I was injured. It actually wasn't such a deep cut, but it bled continuously. We found antiseptic and some bandages in his first aid kit and I was patched up. My wife by this stage was telling me to keep my hand up high to stop the bleeding. So as we left the store with no purchase, I felt like a tour leader, my hand held up over my head, red bandage waving in the wind, as we proceeded to walk down the 200 steps to get to our dinner.

After further research, I have come to the conclusion that the wedding market may not be ideal one to target. Medical tourism, on the other hand, now that might be something to consider.

Dear Diary,

Something a little different this week as I have been looking back at some of my old journals. I used to write a series of entries called *Random Thoughts* and I thought I would share a few of my cerebral sentiments with you, especially as this is the year that keeps on giving:

I believe that absence does **not** make the heart grow fonder
and that time does **not** heal all wounds.
It is time that makes the heart grow fonder
and absence that heals all wounds.

I believe that we always forgive the beautiful ones no matter how ugly their actions.

I believe apologies come to the lips
of those who have nothing left to say.

I believe it's hard not to place the blame when it is so easy to do.

I believe the end of the beginning
is also the beginning of the end.

I believe that you can share one's history,
impact on their today,
yet still be absent from their future.

I believe you should always be wary of memories,
for they often bite the heart that feed them.

I believe an extrovert is nothing more than an introvert
going to extremes to conceal their true self.

I believe that one should always expect the worst;
it makes the inevitable easier to bear
and the unexpected more momentous.

I believe you can live your life
and still have time to find your dreams.

Of course, the opposite of *random* is *modnar* and strangely enough, that makes more sense than most of 2020.

And although the world will be a little different once we can travel freely again, we will still be able to live our lives and find our dreams.

Dear Diary,

I once heard that you should always finish what you have started and unless you mean to do another harm, I tend to agree.

Last week, I was overwhelmed by the response to some of my fractured logic, so this week I have decided to share the remainder of my *Random Thoughts* series with you:

I believe the most dangerous time is when I am alone,
for that is when I have time to think.

I believe we often fear life itself because of our own mortality.

I believe I possess a plethora of masks,
some pliable, some stained,
yet all worn to protect my very soul.

I believe that love is a rally of banners and marches.

I believe a foreign tongue resonates like a symphonic interlude,
the lyrical melody of a hidden rhapsody.

I believe my past has no future,
it only has a memory.

I believe a second thought is often a conscious one,
just as the truth is often a secret.

I believe that to bleed is to feel,
to cry is to breathe,
to love is to live.

I believe that the shadow cast from the rim of my hat
will be the coldest I shall ever endure.

I believe that this is the first day of the rest of my life.

I have been buoyed by the progress of scientists from all around
the world working on finding a vaccine; and despite some incessant
bumps in the road, I can finally see a light at the end of the
proverbial tunnel.

So make sure that you too make this the first day of the rest of your
life.

Dear Diary,

Inspiration can be found in many forms and for me personally, music has always been at the top of that list. I listen to music to motivate, to provoke, to celebrate, to dream and I regard it as my muse. In fact, if you have ever bumped into me on a flight or in an airport lounge, you most likely have seen me wearing headphones, bopping along and singing to myself.

This week I watched *Letter To You* on Apple TV+, which is an introspective account of the recording of the new Bruce Springsteen album of the same name. I have noticed that over the last several years, he has embraced this style of storytelling and created many similar narratives. Springsteen has an amazing voice both vocally and intellectually, yet I am definitely a late bloomer in the fan department as it has only been over the last 10-15 years that I have truly begun to appreciate his talent. What I am certain has helped is that my go-to album on any long-haul flight is a Springsteen compilation album. The first track is *Rosalita*, which instantly sends good vibes and helps me drift off to sleep.

In 2014, Springsteen came to town on his High Hopes Tour. I had forever read about what an amazing showman he was on stage so decided that this would be the year to test these claims first-hand. The concert also became my birthday present as his shows were around the same date. He ironically performed at Hope Estate in the Hunter Valley and as this was a last-minute decision, I was only able to purchase some very (very) inflated tickets on Viagogo. The next thing was to try and find accommodation, which was nigh impossible; but I ended up finding a place in Toronto, which was almost an hour away. I remember that at the beginning of the concert he walked out into the crowd and started taking home-made signs off his fans. I thought this was a little strange but quickly realised that this was would become his impromptu set list for the evening, interspersed with tracks from the *High Hopes* album. Three hours later and I was a believer. The hype was real. So much so that we turned around and did it all again in 2017, this time with friends, when he toured once more. Again we found ourselves at Hope Estate, but with accommodation much (much) closer; and not even a hail storm during the concert could deter us.

I have been extremely fortunate over the years and have had the pleasure of attending many concerts, including The Rolling Stones, U2, Phil Collins, Billy Joel, Metallica, Slipknot, KISS, Living Colour, Barry White, Andrea Bocelli, Barbara Streisand, Interpol, Tracy Chapman, Ed Sheeran, Lianne La Havas, to name but a few. I even took my daughter to see One Direction, which is a debt that can never (ever) be repaid in just one lifetime.

Yet I would rank Springsteen in my Top 3 concerts of all-time, and he slots in neatly at #2.

#3 would be Stevie Wonder. I only ever saw him live once, and that was in 1987 when I was just 14yo (yes, you can do the maths if you want). Prior to the concert, I remember we somehow met one of his back-up singers (Keith John) at a diner on George Street which may or may not have been City Extra. If my memory serves me right, there was a group who entered wearing satin tour jackets and we got talking to them. I definitely remember that we ended up with his autograph on a paper napkin, which made my sister's evening as she thought he was super cute. So much excitement, and all this was prior to the actual concert.

Performing in the round at the Sydney Entertainment Centre, Stevie was just amazing. This was his *Characters* Tour and his voice and musicianship were awe-inspiring. He played the keyboards and the drums, but for most of the night he sat in front of his piano playing hit after hit as the stage slowly kept rotating around. This included all the songs from the new album, but also so many of his old 'Little' Stevie Motown hits, as well as songs from his epic *Hotter Than July* album. I remember that his spoken monologue about abolishing apartheid and freeing Mandela sent shivers down my teenage spine with messages of hope and understanding that still ring true today. At one point, he got so excited that he stood up and climbed up onto the stool he was sitting on. This sent all his stage hands in a panic and they ended up surrounding him, standing all around his piano at the ready should he fall.

#1, well, that has to be Prince. There are not enough superlatives to describe his genius. I have every album he ever released, officially and unofficially. Suffice to say I have always been a fan and if I was ever stranded on a desert island with the music from just one artist to listen to for the rest of my living days, Prince would get the nod. He toured Australia four times and I was lucky enough to see him on each occasion: 1992, 2003, 2012 and 2016. Each time was amazing and different but his second tour, billed as a *Greatest Hits* Tour, remains my favourite. By 2003, I was a fully-fledged member of his New Power Generation Music Club, an interactive website which gave members exclusive content. I also purchased my concert tickets through the website, which guaranteed me seats within the first 10 rows at the Sydney Entertainment Centre. It also pays to have friends at Ticketek because just like that, I was front row centre.

The experience began by getting to the venue some three hours prior to the event, to pick up some exclusive merchandise. Next was the pre-concert sound check. This lasted over an hour, was limited to just 300 people, and Prince casually walked around, chatted, sang and played every instrument on stage. You could have sent me home then and there and I would have been happy. The main concert lasted for almost three hours. Hit after hit after hit. And then it was off to The Basement for an after-concert party which lasted another couple of hours.

As the main concert began, I remember a security guard leaning over and playfully asking my wife whether she was one of his crazy fans that he had to be wary of. She simply pointed to me and said that I was the one to keep an eye on. At one point during the concert, Prince invited fans up on stage. Being front row centre and a gentleman, I helped my wife on stage first, but just as I was ready to get up, I got blocked by a rush of people. It was like being in Las Vegas at the buffet line when someone yells out that the crab claws are about to run out. So there I was, looking up at my wife standing on stage right next to Prince. How could the world be so cruel? I mean OK, you could argue that she 'might' have a better voice than me, but I definitely have the better dance moves by far. Fast forward to 2012 and the *Welcome 2* Tour at Qudos Bank Arena, where we once again found ourselves near the front of the stage. I got speaking to some fellow fans and I found out the name of the song when he normally invites fans up. Here was my chance to right the wrong of nine years ago. As that particular song began, we made our way to the designated spot and just like last time, I helped my wife on stage. And just like last time, you guessed it, I got blocked again. This time he even handed my wife a tambourine to play, and I swear he did a double take because he recognised her.

CHAPTER 9
DECEMBER

Dear Diary,

I wanted to warn you that next week, I shall not be sharing with you any of my weekly thoughts.

It's not because you have upset me in any way or that we have drifted apart. And I think you have realised by now that it's certainly not because I have run out of things to say. It is simply by virtue of the fact that next week, I will be away.

You see, sometime later today, I intend to board a plane for the very first time since the end of February, and travel just a little further than my Laundry or any of the other exotic locations I discovered months ago during lockdown. Destination = Tasmania.

My first ever trip to Hobart was almost 20 years ago for a site visit, and I landed late at night and was in town for less than 24 hours. So I think it would be safe to say that my first real visit to our southernmost state was in 2017. The funny thing is, I never really wanted to go. Let me rephrase that: Tasmania had been on my bucket list but only when I grew much (much) older. For whatever reason, I had always thought of the Apple Isle as a destination for old people. Somewhere you went to retire or visited after you had retired. And as I (still) think of myself as a spritely young thing, that meant it was never a priority and that I had other destinations I wanted to experience first.

Well, that all changed after returning from one of my regular sales trips to India. My trips to India are always incredible, rewarding and worthwhile, but upon my return, I often find myself drained and feeling a little precious. So once I was home, somewhere between unpacking my suitcase and loading the washing machine with my unmentionables, I was informed that flights to Tasmania had been booked and paid for during the September school holidays.

Great. Now I would have to put in for leave, organise all of the accommodation, hire a car, do research, yadda yadda yadda.

So how many days were we staying for? Seven. Seven? Seven days! That's way too long. Surely we would only need 3-4 days to see everything of note.

I could not have been more wrong. The more I researched and asked questions, the more there was to discover. Tasmania is a foodie's paradise and produces vast quantities of quality meat, seafood and honey, to name but a few provisions. Its natural landscape is stunning, full of jagged mountains, gushing waterfalls and welcoming bays.

We settled on staying in Hobart, Launceston and Freycinet.

From Hobart we did day trips to Port Arthur and MONA (Museum of Old and New Art). One must also pay a visit to the Salamanca Market; it's a vibrant outdoor melange of stalls showcasing the best the state has to offer, from food to drink to crafts to art to music.

From Launceston we discovered the Tamar Valley and George Town. It is also home to the stunningly beautiful Cataract Gorge and Basin, which is literally a short stroll from the city centre. A picturesque lunch spot if there ever was one.

From Freycinet we loved Coles Bay and the stunning East Coast. Freycinet National Park is visually spectacular and has many walks for novices and experienced hikers alike.

And all along our journey we were spoilt for choice by the amazing wineries on hand, housing some world class Pinot Noir, and the abundance of gin, vodka and whisky distilleries which are now being lauded all over the world. In fact, I was so enamoured by the whisky that I decided to buy my own private barrel with a friend, which was only recently bottled. Called *Pareve and Co*, it is a single malt in a sherry cask which is the nectar of the gods. You won't find it for sale anywhere but if you are interested, I know some people.

I came to the realisation that Tasmania is absurdly self-sufficient and I truly believe that if there was ever a nuclear apocalypse, Tasmania would survive. Perhaps the pandemic has tested that theory somewhat this year, but I still believe in my hypothesis. You only have to look at the resiliency of the incredibly cute and disturbing Tasmanian Devil as an example. The recent news that they were released into a sanctuary on the mainland goes to show that it must be a great place to live and regenerate. And I also like to think that roaming somewhere amongst the rugged landscape is a Tasmanian Tiger or two, and that they made the decision to go into hiding years ago until the world got itself in order. Sadly, they are still waiting to make their long-waited return.

I will admit, I am also excited to simply visit an airport and fly on a plane again. And a little nervous. So I was extremely lucky to be able to get in some much needed practice when I was invited to attend a client Christmas Party earlier this week.

So that they would be completely Covid compliant and assure the safety of all their staff and passengers, boarding times were staggered throughout the day. As we entered the aircraft we were greeted by the Captain and her crew. Refreshments were served throughout our flight, and although the road was a little rocky, the quiches and chicken sandwiches made up for that. I was even able to wet my whistle with some cheeky bubbles. And I was thrilled to find out that they still had some inflight entertainment, complete with a country Cinderella, and the irony was not lost on me that she was still wearing her canvas slippers.

So the moral of the story, then, is to not put off today what you may never do tomorrow. There is delight to be found in the unexpected. And never (ever) take life for granted.

Dear Diary,

I'm back!

Tasmania was invigorating, brilliant, exciting and relaxing all at the same time. Apart from a few hiccups – yes, I am looking at you, Jetstar, and your multiple departure time changes followed by our return flight cancellation – my trip was just what my travel agent ordered.

And I am also very glad to report that I returned in one piece and in good health.

I am aware that I most likely posted way too much detail about my trip on social media but I couldn't help myself, I was just so thrilled to be travelling again. I think part of me also wanted my posts to become some sort of public service announcement to remind my modest following about the joys of travel and to show that the time is right to begin new adventures. And that now is the time to dust off those suitcases, lay out your active wear flight ensemble, practise those shocked and distraught looks when your luggage comes in over the limit at check-in, interrogate your friends for restaurant recommendations, seek out those money-can't-buy experiences, and get out there and discover what we have in our own backyard. And with a bit of luck, it won't be long until we will be tearing the house upside-down again, searching for our passports because we will be heading overseas once more.

I also wanted to let you all know that this will be my last Dear Diary entry. It's hard to believe that I sent my very first one way back on March 18th, when I simply wanted to reach out and see how everyone was coping. It then took a sharp left turn somewhere along the way, and nine months later I was left talking about my pyjamas, Dr Seuss, Halloween and my Laundry.

So a very BIG and SINCERE thank you to everyone who indulged me along the way.

Thank you also to everyone who called just to have a chat.

Thank you also to everyone who emailed just to say hello.

And thank you to everyone who interacted with me every week.

I know that many of you just pressed 'Delete' whenever I happened to slide into your Inbox, but the fact that I only received three *Unsubscribe* requests was encouraging. I think that might even mean I wasn't boring the majority of you with my words.

So no matter what or how you celebrate over this period, I wish you good health, good vibes, prosperity, and above all, an event-free couple of weeks.

In the meantime, I pray that you stay safe, sane and healthy.

And until next time, Diary, keep washing those hands.

Author's Note

The irony is, I have always wanted to publish a book, yet on this occasion, it was never my motivation.

Returning to Australia from India on February 29th, 2020, little did I realise that this would be (as of writing) my last trip abroad.

Throughout the month of March, as the severity of COVID-19 began to sink in, I felt compelled to reach out to as many of our clients and partners as possible, just to check in on their wellbeing.

So I started emailing them and by April 08th, 2020, these had somehow morphed into the *Dear Diary* series that you see today.

I initially had concerns that I would simply be an unwelcomed addition to their Inbox but was genuinely overwhelmed by the number of phone calls, emails and messages I received in reply.

Some just wanted to chat, some shared with me their own stories, while others just wanted to thank me for reaching out.

Yet I should have been thanking them, for their inspiration allowed me to relive adventures I had not thought about for years.

Travel is indeed a privilege and one that should never be taken for granted.

Acknowledgements

Thank you to my wife and daughter for always putting up with me and my moods. We can always see the stars, the sun, the moon.

Thank you to my work colleagues who indulged me and encouraged me.

Thank you to everyone who read me on a weekly basis and shared with me your own crazy, absurd and hilarious stories which put mine to shame.

Parris Fotias was born in the Blue Mountains just west of Sydney and loves to travel, loves to write and loves professional wrestling.

Parris received a bachelor of arts in communications from the University of Western Sydney where he studied writing as part of his degree. After graduating, he had several articles published as both a sports and travel freelance journalist.

By day he works as Regional Sales Director for a legendary hotel brand, fighting a never ending battle for lounge access, aisle seats and Frequent Flyer points.

In his spare time, Parris writes poetry, prose and short stories. His style has been described as both dark and observational, exploring the intricacies and complexities of relationships throughout life; with family, friends, lovers and with ones' self.

Adventures Through COVID: The Art of Subconscious Travel in a Transcendental State is Parris' first book

* 9 7 8 1 9 2 2 6 2 9 5 6 2 *